ILLUMINATED BY LOVE

ILLUMINATED BY LOVE

A Journey into Your True Self

Devaji

ISBN: 978-1-7326813-0-9 (paperback)

Editors: Ana Ramana and Janis Harper

Front Cover Photo: Ramana Spencer

Back Cover Photo: Martin Caulley

Interior Photos: Madhu, Amrita Brummel-Smith

Book Jacket Design: Madhu and Alex Macintyre

Book Design and Layout: Aaron Rose, Mount Shasta, California

Published by In the Heart of Silence, www.devaji.org

Dedication

The offering of these pages is dedicated to my wife Faith, who has been an ongoing support, inspiration, and companion on this journey. She embodies the silence, love, and compassion of a true sage.

Everyone is always
looking for love

The wildest love affair
the life has ever known
lies dormant within you

Just to let the whispers
of the Beloved
sing in your Heart

An Invitation to the Reader

Given the profound transmission that moves through Devaji's talks, it is recommended that you approach this book slowly and with care. Perhaps the richest pearls can be extracted by absorbing a couple of pages at a time so you can fully imbibe the depth of the offering.

The first and final sections of *Illuminated by Love* address the connection to and communion with the Absolute. They explore the nature of love and truth. These chapters cushion a series of more instructional monologues, offering guidance on particular issues that may arise on the path home to your true Self.

However you approach these pages, may the grace of true wisdom be your guide.

Contents

1. Receiving the Nectar

11. Transforming Obstacles into Grace

III. Embracing the Spiritual Warrior

IV. The Doorway into Your Self

V. The Path Back Home

VI. The Mystical Taste

Acknowledgments

I would first and foremost like to offer my profound thanks to Ana Ramana, who not only edited but selected, arranged, and created the flavor of this book. She was assisted throughout the process by Janis Harper, to whom I'm also hugely grateful for putting in long hours of dedicated service editing the manuscript. I'd also like to thank Nalini Davison, Sandy Leader, and Karen Osborne for their contributions to the completion of this book. Great appreciation also to the many transcribers who helped usher this book into being. My deep joy and appreciation goes out to the entire sangha. This is a unique community of people who have offered their lives in the service of Truth and Freedom. The blossoming of the light, love, and communion that has arisen here is far beyond what could ever have been imagined. I would also like to honor my daughter, Malaena, whose journey has been dedicated to spreading the light.

Intoxicated

What is there to search for?

Soar like a wild bird up into the infinite sky
Sing your song where there are no ears to hear you
Do your ecstatic dance where there are no eyes to see you
Meet in the secret sanctuary that lives inside of you

Come and celebrate here
as the beauty of this light desires
to express itself

What difference does this body make?
It cannot touch, or scar, or alter anything

What difference does the play of time make?
It is merely a shadow

It is your sacred heart that is the whisperer of truth
for only your ears

Just receive its grace

Live intoxicated with this beauty

Welcome Home

In the human heart there exists a deep yearning and pain to reunite in pure love. Every one of us was disillusioned in some way with the conditional love that was felt in our families. And rightly so, because in truth this is not the love that you were seeking. How could it measure up to that which you know inside your heart to be true love, the union with your Beloved? Every heart holds the memory of this pure, ecstatic love.

Of course you've been searching for that, but in all the wrong places, in places where it cannot be found. You've been searching for the love externally that has lived deep within your own heart all along, undiscovered because of looking outward. The beauty of this journey is that it finds you again. In the reunion with the Beloved, the Beloved finds you. All that it wants is you.

Your true heart goes beyond the things that you love, beyond all the expressions of joy that are part of the character: the love of nature, birds, poetry, solitude. These can feel so sacred and so connected—but still you exist beyond even that. The love that you are transcends all that separates out one thing in favor of something else. Of course there is nothing wrong with any particular expression of love. The expression of love is beautiful, but it is not the totality of who you are.

At some point you will be freed of absolutely everything—every preference, every perspective, every bit of knowingness. Here is the reunion of love that the character has always searched for: the absolute, complete, and total envelopment that is timeless and never-ending, that never judges or abandons you. Here is the total immersion into Love itself, where there is no you and other. You are totally merged, like the raindrop falling into the ocean, knowing beyond reason that everything else was never real.

Every heart has emerged from this one Love, and every heart has been longing to be home again. All the great mystics realized the same thing that we know to be true deep down: you are what you've been searching for. Rest in what your heart itself knows to be true. Have compassion for the wandering human mind looking for its true love in all the wrong places.

Every place in the heart that was hurt in that search folded upon itself. In opening to this moment, in trusting in the true nature of your heart here and now, all that has folded begins to unfold like a blossoming flower. It is its natural way—just allowing, witnessing, being. There is no one in control. Every moment is unfolding perfectly, and the heart is finding its true love again. It's what everyone has always really wanted. It's what everyone knows somewhere inside. It's the true nature of love.

All disturbances have been acquired. All external distractions have been conditioned. There is not one heart that does not arise out of this pure beauty. There is not one heart that will not return to this. Let everything hidden come up that wants to be seen or felt, that wants to unfurl, so that your true love is revealed. Then what would you search for in this life? What would you need? In this union with your own heart, with the Beloved, everything unfolds absolutely perfectly, unfiltered, un-fettered by the containing and bottling up. The doors begin to swing wide open.

Wouldn't you give everything up for this—every fear, every sub-stitute desire? Everyone is welcome. There are no exceptions. Everyone is welcome back home. Let us sit in the knowingness of assured reunion with the Beloved. When the mind starts to speak, know it for what it is: just the mind doing its thing.

You cannot force the heart open any more than you can force a flower to open. It's all being orchestrated. Your heart is opening in its own perfect time, and you are free to stop micromanaging

God's unfolding of its own heart. Let everything come back to perfect peace in honoring the one Heart that patiently waits within.

1.
Receiving the Nectar

God has been Seeking You

I'd like to pass on something to you that came through the silence.

There is no need to seek. There is no need to look for me.

The experience of personal doing, of personal effort, is what prevents me from finding you. Simply remove habitual distractions. Recognize that I am in every single thing. In every sound, generating every thought. Creating everything seen, creating the seer, creating the experience of action, the experience of doer-ship.

When there is simply stopping and a humble readiness to just meet me, you discover that I am everything. It is not a seeking; it is a recognition that there is nothing I am not. And then my search for you is over.

The search is my job, not yours. Yours is just to receive me. So simple.

It is only when you are in habitual distraction, lost in the illusion of my absence, that I cannot find you. I am breathing your body, thinking what are called your thoughts. I am the perceiver and the objects perceived. It is just a question of receiving me.

Be still and receive me.

How to Fall in Love

Teaching about what is called "enlightenment" is kind of like teaching someone how to fall in love. It is absurd, because falling in love is not mental. But what you can teach is how to release the conditioned habits that cause you to close down so that you are not available to receive true intimacy. This can be taught.

The nature of conditioned mind is that it is built to fear intimacy. It craves intimacy but it also fears it. The experience of separation is that of being separate from the deepest intimacy possible, which is so huge that the individual one is lost in the sea of absolute Love. And everything conditioned is built around a fear of just that. "What will become of me? What about my job, my responsibilities, what about tomorrow?" If this journey is merely a passionate hobby, one does not face these fears. But if you are committed all the way, you will absolutely face conditioned terror, all built around the experience of being separate from the falling into this indescribable Love.

In the kindness of the way the play works, almost everyone at some point tastes the flush of new infatuation, the taste of falling in love. This occurs because, temporarily, the ego-mind creates in what looks to be another all that it has perceived as being missing from "me." For a moment, the conditioned mind relaxes, and joy and love flower.

But if it arises from something external, it is short-lived. It is only a tiny taste of the depth of what is revealed when the shell of separation is shattered. It is not falling in love with someone or something. It is Love falling wildly, drunkenly in love with itself, which is everything. It sees only the one Love that appears in everything. And its relationship is a complete and totally ecstatic love affair.

Yet everything that conditioned mind has created is built around the fear of letting go of being separate, of the experience of "me." And this is what all of the teaching is about. It is what all of the challenge is about: dismantling what created the armoring.

And the beauty of the way this dreamscape is set up is that it is tailor-constructed to unravel the experience of the separate one. Every dreamer in his or her own dream is constantly being offered the perfect gift in perfect timing to unravel every element. This can only happen when there is the simple readiness to let go of the conditioned attempt to control, to let go of the habit of running, and just to receive.

And what is meant by "receive"? It is receiving the totality of what is playing. It is not the character receiving its apparent external environment; it is receiving the whole dream. And what receives the dream is what is aware of the dream. And what is aware of the dream is what is present. What is present is what is unchanging. From this, there is clear seeing. The moment this is tasted it becomes so clear that all of the elements that come forth in the dreamscape are perfectly set up to unravel all that created the experience of bondage.

There is no future in it. Future is the habit of running away from what is. There is no past in it. Past is the habit of running away from the offer that is. There is nothing to know. Knowing something is built out of the fear of not knowing. It is just to be open, to remain still, to witness what is at play.

What is being spoken about is not a doing. Doing only arises when one has fallen away from what is present. Simply remain still and receive the grace, and witness the mind's response. Be aware of all that is playing. See from where it is coming.

Infatuation

When the veil is thin
When everything conditioned is unconditioned
When the reflection is a clear slate

When the tendencies that were familiar
have evaporated
and movement is spontaneous

What is rediscovered is the state of infatuation

It is like rediscovering the innocence of a child
but it is infused with ancient wisdom

It is more mature than time
More childlike than an infant

And it no longer requires effort

Just like early infatuation
it is impossible to remove yourself
from this feeling of in-love-ness

And it is in love with the divine
that lives inside your heart

The Love Affair

In the beginning, the experience of the individualized conditioned ego goes on a search, which is in itself grace. But the ego's point of reference is limited to that which language can speak. As one becomes ripe, there arises a willingness to release what has perpetuated the experience of being someone separate.

On the one hand, it is simple. And on the other, it is the greatest possible challenge of a human life. The conditioned perspective is built for survival. And survival means not allowing oneself to be vulnerable. These very protective mechanisms prevent the taste of this love affair, which transcends anything that the mind-body will ever know.

So there begins the birth of true humility, which is the willingness to put down the armor and to receive the offer just as it is, whatever it is, recognizing that it is coming out of true wisdom. It is arising out of this pure Love that, in fact, is longing for you.

The word "silence" is often considered the absence of sound, but it has nothing to do with whether sound is appearing or not. It is the feeling of silence—the feeling of oneness, of what has not been broken into pieces by protection born of fear. It is the feeling in your heart, the beauty that is alive now. It is not felt somewhere; it is felt everywhere. It is, in fact, the nature of your existence. Your existence is now. It is always *now*. How could it not be now? You've never existed for a second in the story of a past or future.

In the beginning it may feel like stillness—like space, equanimity, peace. But when there is true ripeness, then you receive the grace that is offered without any attempt to control or manipulate. Then you discover that grace has orchestrated the unraveling of the box of "me."

What begins to arise is what the mind calls "vulnerability." You find yourself falling in love with the aliveness of the awakening heart. And out of this aliveness is the birth of the taste of the true love affair. It is an intoxication that can never be spoken. Gradually the mystical taste is revealed, not for a select few but as the natural state of things.

You find yourself wildly in love with everything. And when I say "you," I am not talking about the mind-body point of reference. I realize that until one is very deeply rooted and mature in this, experience is dictated by how the reference point is doing, swinging between expansion and contraction. It's like the breath. You cannot have the exhalation without the inhalation.

Expansion is when everything that is desired is experienced from the point of reference. It's when the reference point believes it experiences love, joy, pleasure, and connectedness with God, and it has a sense of well-being in the body and quietness of mind. And then there comes the contractive phase, where everything the mind fears presents itself, and the story is "something is wrong." And it oscillates back and forth between the two.

Freedom is freedom from the point of reference. What is called "awakening" is awakening to the nature of your very existence, which is prior to the birth of time. It is impossible for the mind to comprehend—but if you know your Self, it is completely self-evident. Your very being lives in unending prostration to a love affair that can never be spoken.

If it is what you really want, it becomes the only thing. If it is the only thing, you are truly graced. And it can't be the only thing if there has not been a taste. But there has been a taste. That's why you're here in satsang. I can give you all kinds of pointers that are helpful to the mind. But the truth is, this wild love is only alive *now*. Future and past are a habit of forgetfulness.

How do you live in the *now?* You must put yourself in the environment that is going to support that. The reason why satsang is offered is because it is an invitation for the one who is hungry. It's not because of me. I arise out of your imagination. Rather it is what I represent.

Relaxing into What Is

Within all of the various teachings, it really comes down to the simplicity of just relaxing. This has nothing to do with the mind-body relaxing, but with relaxation itself. This means re-laxing into whatever is playing. You discover that relaxation is unchanging, whereas the mind-body is all over the map.

From the mind-body orientation, there is a straining to feel peace—but that orientation is the straining itself. It is just part of the system that is always oscillating from opening to closing, from appearance to disappearance. But relaxation remains the same. Eventually, through all of the various changes, that which is relaxed shifts from the background to the foreground.

This occurs by remembering that hypnosis has convinced you to be you, and you are nothing more than ever-changing oscil-lations. Every time an oscillation occurs can be a reminder to just relax. Relax and feel the peace. This is not a peace that is dependent on anything that cycles in the body. Relaxation is what is in the moment—in *this* moment. If there is struggle, let that be a reminder not to struggle more aggressively, but to see that attention has been pulled into distraction.

This too is choiceless. Just simply trust and relax and let the deeper wisdom have free rein. You soon discover that even when the body is miserable, this peace cannot leave you. It is your nature. You cannot know it as your nature until you recognize when the tendency is too strong to forget. This is the grace of the contracted phase.

If there is any struggle, relax. Let it be. Then immediately there is a taste of what is unaffected. Eventually you'll begin to discover that you are in fact unaffected by the body, no matter what it is doing. You see how it completely governed your experience until you began shaking off the amnesia. Everything that seemed so important becomes irrelevant.

And deeper still, you start to see that it is all being taken care of by grace. Re-identification with your story can be a reminder to just relax. It is all being carried. Don't look for the tension to relax. Simply relax *into* the tension. Relax into everything. Relax into what is everywhere, into your Self. Ease into what is eternally present, the timeless nature of peace that is always present.

Mind may want to hold on to some concern. This is no problem. Just relax. It is all under divine guidance. The doer is a myth. Let the habitual relationship with body relax. Let habitual relationship with mind relax. Notice the habits that want your attention, and remember just to relax. It is all being taken care of. There is no individual to do anything. It is all working in perfect order.

Future is a mental contrivance; there is no such thing. Doing is a mental contrivance; there is no such thing. In reality none of it is impacting you. What matters to mind is meaningless. Not some of it, not most of it—all of it. Sink into this deep relaxation, this deep peace, the unchanging nature of what is.

Turn the Breath Over

Feel the breath like the waves of the ocean
receiving its grace and then falling deeper
into the unchanging essence
of your eternal nature

Free the burden of any illusion
of doing the breath
Turn the breath over

When the breath is turned over
the body is turned over
when the body is turned over
you are liberated

When you are liberated
the unmoving essence
that is closer than the breath
and more intimate than the body
is what remains

Holy Mother: The Path to Joy

I'd like to share a message of grace from the Holy Mother that came through for you.

You, as a character, cannot approach me. You as you are, which is pure joy, receives me. The only way you can truly receive me is when you are living in your Self, which is simply this unbroken joy.

Consistently living in the joy that is your true nature requires complete humility, because the nature of suffering is actually the strongest force in the play of separation. It so aggressively wants to draw attention onto itself. It takes humility to let go of the habit of being drawn into the surface veneer and to simply recognize the inherent nature of pure joy that is, in fact, who you are. The character cannot get there no matter how hard it efforts. Humility lies in the release of misery and the resultant recognition of pure happiness. It is where you and I are one.

And then at the times when the apparent character is in misery, it becomes like a comic strip: laughable. When there is recognition that the deepest humility in life is simply living in the joy that is your nature, then you truly receive me. Receiving me is not only the greatest beauty and liberation for you, but it is also the deepest offering to me. It is the deepest offering that is possible. It is seva *in its truest form.*

Feel the inherent joy that is unbounded, and then I can find you. Live unwaveringly in this joy, and then discover that I am you. Hold the unbroken humility to release relationship with suffering, no matter what its story may be, no matter how intense the pull may be, no matter how aggressive the conditioning may be.

Pure unalloyed joy—it is the undercurrent of reality. The humility to let go of suffering is the doorway where I lie waiting for you.

11.
Transforming Obstacles into Grace

The Formation of Ego

I would like to look at what creates the ego, because it is not possible to have a full understanding of the dismantling process without assimilating how it is formed.

In very early life, there is the experience of either subtle or overt tensions. This may begin in the embryo, but certainly once birth occurs this is almost always the immediate experience. When these clashing energies arise, a numbing protective shell comes in to soften this sudden intensity, like a warrior's armoring. This armoring alleviates the energetic friction and numbs the intensity, but it also numbs all feeling and creates the experience of someone who is separate.

What creates this shell are the interactive dynamics that are present in early childhood—and this is what I refer to as "the construct," "the imprint." It is all created by an interactive dynamic, not by one separate being. It is the relationship of Mommy to Daddy, Mommy to me, Daddy to me, siblings, and friends, that give rise to the nature of the shell, which then causes the formation of the personality that experiences life as "me." The personality is created through all of these influences.

Out of the birth of this shell is the experience of "me" and the experience of "other." The shell itself has created the particulars about me, what feels familiar, what I like and don't like, what feels safe and unsafe. It is like a seamless piece of glass that cannot even be discerned because it is unbroken. And then, upon birth, it is dropped and broken into all of these fragments. The biggest fragment is me, the one who has built the shell, the one who then experiences all of the emotions and thoughts and perspectives. The second and third biggest pieces are usually Mommy and Daddy, and then the pieces get smaller. But what has been fragmented remains broken and is kept safe and tucked away under the armor.

And then there is this maneuvering in life to get away from those influences that caused the initial shattering and resultant armoring. There is an attempt to always stay away from the conflicts that caused the need for protection. And yet no matter how hard you try, they replay over and over again, causing what the mind defines as "problems in life."

So every player sees itself as the focal one and everything else as "other." They go into meditation where the others are not there and it feels safe. They can do the internal work, which is of great importance. This removes the habit of distraction; it slows the patterning and spinning of mind, which is driven by trying to get away from everything internal. Now you can begin to meet these inner pieces that you have been constantly running away from.

But there is also a role in the dream itself. If there is true surrender, then every stimulus that is defined by mind as "external" becomes an avenue to meet the internal reactivity. When this meeting is true and whole, it is seen that this reactivity has just been looking for that which can hold it, that which does not abandon it. The external stimulus brings up the internal pieces that created the armor.

This originally occurred because the experience was of there being no safe haven. But now you are the safe haven, and the external stimulus becomes the vehicle to meet the internal condition. Each time it is used this way, something that formed the shell is dissolved by love. As this occurs, you begin to feel the continuous nature of external and internal, how it is all your perception. It is not broken; it is a continuum.

There is a deeper trust of things, a deeper opening into everything. It becomes so clear that nothing new ever happens, that all issue is internal. What is external stimulus only sets off internal reaction, and the internal reaction is always old. It becomes obvious that what is perceived to be external is only perception. It is actually coming from buried internal turbulence that was hidden by this protective armor, which created the experience that you are separate. But every time the external play offers the grace that it is always offering, some internal element is healed and freed and released, and the armoring begins to dissolve on its own.

Eventually all of the fragmented pieces begin to coalesce. What was broken begins feeling whole. What was external begins to be felt as your Self. Inside and outside begin to fall away. What was permeating the whole dream becomes the flavor, and it is pure beauty. At this point the human aspect, that which was broken and ignorant and hidden, becomes complete.

It is like a child of yours who is ready to go away to college, as opposed to you sending your child away because they are making you miserable. The ego is not a getting away from; it is a making whole. When it is whole, it disappears on its own. In this natural movement, the love affair that is driving everything, that is overflowing into everything, becomes wildly alive.

There is nothing to search for. There is nowhere to go. You see that the one Source is everywhere, in everything, all of the time. There is no one left to do anything. And then there is the taste of peace and joy, infused with love, which is the passion that brings everything to light.

Then meditation is not defined by what someone is doing. It is the constant attitude of being. And now that the walls have broken apart, each time some player moves into your sphere who is in great suffering, the pain is imbibed. And in this, something burns deeper that opens the doorway even more.

Initially it was about meeting what was called your "broken

41

pieces." But eventually one becomes the vessel that welcomes the broken pieces of all humanity. And each time they are met and received and taken in, something becomes more whole. And in this wholeness, the taste of passion and love and beauty ignites more deeply. What was once the separate self is absorbed by the heart of eternity. And there is falling into the Absolute.

When the Heart is Broken Open

When the egoic shell of separation is in place, one does not feel the subtler levels of the pain of going against your Self. Nor is it recognized that every single action arising out of "have to, need to, should" stems from the mind's fear. These subtler elements go unnoticed, and life becomes automatic. A very familiar sense is formed of "who I am," and "what I like and don't like."

When one is willing to really receive what is being offered—to stop the automatic running and receive—then the numbing mechanism, the wall, the ego, begins to thin. And as it thins, one becomes more sensitive, feeling things more acutely, feeling the love and the perfection and the beauty. Feeling the pain that created the shell as it now melts away. Feeling the innocence of humanity, and at the same time the birthing of your own divinity. Feeling the fragile nature of the human condition inside your own being, all the way through, with such unspeakable tenderness, so big it can break you apart. And at the very same time, the breaking apart opens the gateway into the deeper sensitivity of connecting with your eternal divine nature.

A true journey like this takes everything and offers everything. When these beautiful, tender, broken nuggets that have been buried deep inside yourself are felt into all the way, the heart is broken wide open, and the sensitivity of who you are is connected into the totality of what is driving everything.

And all that has been buried inside, which caused the perception of "me and other," is now transformed and can invite all expressions of life into itself. The tenderness, the meeting, the fragility, the beauty, the vulnerability of the human condition, does not stop. It grows. And the taste of what is vulnerable to nothing grows, what is free of everything—wildly ecstatic and alive and unbound. The more you feel into the human element, the more the heart of God reveals itself.

The Breath of Life

I'd like to speak about relationship with the breath and the release of the habit of doing. It has been spoken often about how the experience of doing arises only when there is a loss of connection with the unchanging feeling of your existence. It doesn't have to be an absolute loss of connection, but it must fall into the background. When the feeling of your unchanging existence is in the foreground, the experience of doing is not possible. It is a phenomenon that appears when there is either a complete loss of connection with your very existence or the connection with your existence is just dwindling in the background.

A great barometer in this process is the breath. Most people almost all the time have the experience that "I am breathing," that the breath is "mine." The breath is such a great tool because it is a complete monitor of the level of tension and the speed of mind. When identification is with mind and it is aggressively moving, the breath will be shallow, short, and rapid. As the process slows down, so too does the breath.

But it is very rare for one to have the direct revelation that the breath itself is coming from the Beloved, that it is in fact the interface between the unmanifest and manifest. It is where the unmanifest breathes life into the play of form. Instead of pulling away from the connection with the feeling of your existence, if you receive the breath it transforms into the most rejuvenating, sensual, internal expression of a love affair—where all sense of "I am doing" melts away, and the revelation is that the body is being breathed.

It is like an internal massage. It is receiving the nectar of the gods when it is recognized for what it is. And then there is the possibility of feeling into from where the breath is coming: the bridge where the unmanifest stillness breathes life into its manifest expression, which receives the grace of the breath of life. And then it is possible to feel what is more immediate, more intimate and closer than the breath, which is the feeling of your Self.

From Where does the Breath Come?

In the simple noticing of the mechanics of breathing, the process of inhaling, taking in, is active. And the process of exhaling is passive. It is a release. Oxygen is what is needed for survival, but the release of what is needed for survival is passive. If there is feeling into the exhaled breath, it is the release of tension.

The feeling of exhaling is actually the feeling of opening because it is a release. It is a feeling of relaxation because it is a release. It is actually letting go. The nature of relationship with mind, with perceptive experience, with everything that is taken in by conditioned mind is like the inhaled breath, and its release is like the exhaled breath.

The release of thought is not active; it is just a letting go, an opening, a relaxation. The release of relationship with sensation is not active; it is a letting go, just like the exhaled breath. The release of the contrivance of a "someone" is like the exhaled breath. What is called vigilance is not active, is not a taking in; it is a release. It is letting go of everything that is perceived to be changing.

The process of release, when you get the feel of it, is such nectar, for it is the release of tension. The inhaled breath is getting something necessary for the experience of survival. It requires the contraction of particular muscles in the body. It is an expenditure of energy—just like everything that is experienced as a mechanism of "my survival." But what the mind calls "active" is passive. What the conditioned mind calls "effort" is the release of effort.

The inhaled breath, if you are conscious of it, feels like a doing.

But the exhaled breath is just happening by itself. This is the nature of the release of every phenomenal experience, a relaxation into just letting go. And just like the breath, both inhaling and exhaling, there is a story that "I am breathing," but it is just happening—otherwise, it would stop in deep sleep.

In the recognition that it is just happening, it is possible to notice what is completely unaffected by the active phase and passive phase, by the movement of survival and its release: that which has no breath, is not in motion, is not of survival or the letting go of conditions of survival. What remains is the feeling of the only thing that is not away from, that is not changing, that is not an object of perception, that is not beginning or ending, not in time or a location.

What occurs when there is falling into what is neither the inhale or the exhale is that the inhaled breath stops becoming active; it stops being infused by this subconscious mechanism of survival. Because, like everything, it is a reflection of the state of awareness, and when there is falling into the nectar that is unchanging, the breath reflects that.

As the feeling of what remains unmoving begins to fall into itself more fully, what can become apparent is from where this breath is coming. When there is no longer a sense of an active phase, and there is simply feeling into, "From where does the breath come? What is doing the breathing?" it can be revealed that the process of inhalation is the unmanifest moving into manifest expression. It is the point of origin of the experience of expression. It is the point of continuation, not separation, like the wave arising in the ocean.

It can reveal how manifest expression and the unmanifest origin (from where the expression arises) are not separate, how the unmanifest is breathing the expression of life. The motion is like the waves in the ocean. The expression is no disturbance. It is beauty. It is only forgetting from where it comes that creates the insanity.

Just remain with your Self, living in the point of inception—the point where Shakti arises out of Shanti, where the wave arises out of the ocean, where the mind arises out of the Self.

Receiving the Beauty

It is such a crazy play. On the one hand, there is this beauty that many recognize. It can be so obvious that it is all benevolence, all kindness and pure love. All the experiences of struggle and darkness, all of the challenges, are just a conditioned overlay. And again and again there is the discovery, in seeing it all the way through, of the undeniable recognition that it is not really staining anything. This beauty is actually illuminating and guiding all of it. It is about nothing but falling in love with that which you are already wholeheartedly devoted to. You do not need to find something. It is already there.

In this seeing, there is the recognition that it is not a doing, because the experience of doing is synonymous with the experience of forgetting. It is all being carried by wisdom. And no matter how the hardships may appear at times, in truth it is all pure kindness. Every single thing. The reason why this journey can seem odd is, at the same time, the conditioned habit is masterful at creating experiences of struggle and effort and failure: those stories that repeat again and again, bringing back the experience of failing in various ways.

The thing is, within the ever-deepening self-recognition lies the knowing that even periods of forgetting are under divine guidance. And it is not required for there to be trust in the process. You already have it. If you turn to your mind, you are turning to the program of deception. But if you really fall into your essence, your heart, it is self-evident: the trust is here, for it is coming from one source. This means that nothing is needed—which doesn't mean that there will not be the appearance of struggle. But what will happen is, as trust deepens, experiences of disturbance become meaningless, no matter the intensity.

At a certain point, the taste of the kindness and beauty will remain unbroken around what is happening. And what remains unbroken remains unchanging. What begins to be discovered is the more the mind-body burns, the greater the beauty—because what is burning is that which has separated and numbed. It is the only thing that can burn. It stops mattering whether the mind is stopped or is active, whether the body is in comfort or discomfort. The active mind is the burning phase, which is burning away numbing.

And then there is the relaxed, restful phase when the mind stops and the body disappears. The openings and closings become like the in-breath and the out-breath, while the essence of your being needs no breath at all. It is not in relationship with breath; it is not in relationship with time. It is the only thing that is not an object away from you. It remains whether the character is distracted or not. Eventually, even when the character is distracted, *you* are not. Inherent within lies a childlike happiness that has never been conditioned.

This love of all things—it is completely free because nothing can disturb it. So there is freedom to fall madly in love without concern or consequence, without relationship with future, without the habit of referring back to a character. Whether experiences are challenging or easeful, it doesn't matter. Whether the story is you are succeeding or failing, they are both just stories.

The stories are illuminated by the wisdom of the recognition that there is really no separate one to succeed or fail. There is the guidance of that which you are in complete devotion to, and it is devotion that is always necessary. It is the one thing not to forget: that the love affair builds upon itself. Hold a humble intention not to turn from your Self.

And then just receive the beauty. How difficult is it to receive beauty? It is all pure joy pouring directly onto you, no matter how it may seem. That is the reality of it. Who could imagine such grace? What a feast!

Your Own Heart

You begin to recognize
Love infuses everything
Your own heart is the wind
It is the trees
It is the earth

It is even the conflicts that arise
It is the pain that comes up

It is the storm
It is the open sky
It is totality

It excludes nothing
And embraces everything

And in this embrace
There is but one taste
And that is the taste
Of Love

Slowing Down

In the play of time, life offers the opportunity to remain in connection with what is timeless. First, however, the life must slow down enough so that there is awareness to receive the appearance of change from the feeling of your being.

The role of life is to constantly bring up challenges, and the mind's relationship to what occurs is a reflection of how connected you are to what is really happening. When the mind is in reaction, it is an indicator that you have fallen away from the true offering. But it is not a problem. The greater the mind's reactivity, the greater the challenge, initially. The challenge is to find from where the mind is coming.

At first, there may be times when it seems impossible. We think, "I've strayed so far from my Self that I'm completely lost in old patterns." This is where vigilance comes in. The challenge is to remain present with what is, even in the face of how it may seem. Remain aware of what is—not what is arising from the mind's interpretation, but what is, no matter what it is. It will become apparent that the nature of life is to throw up every potential situation in order to create and sustain old habits of distraction. But you cannot be free until you are free of these conditioned habits.

As you begin to seek to discover from where the mind is coming, as opposed to following the content of the mind's story, the nature of thoughts will begin to change. However, if the seeking is driven by the desire for the thoughts to change, it cannot work.

So you remain vigilant, even with processes that the mind does not like, those things that are in opposition to the conditioned mind's desire system. In this vigilance, the mind's impact begins to lose its power. The thought complexes that arise begin to soften and shift. What begins to be noticed at times of challenge is that the mind's nature shifts from being in opposition to being in submission.

There is a shift from a story that is perpetuating suffering to seeing from where these thoughts are coming. And then there pours forth gratitude and beauty, along with the recognition that every single thing, no matter what it is, has just been a test. The test has been created out of a wisdom that holds the potential of intensifying your conviction. So everything that seemed to be an issue is recognized as a doorway—revealing that when something seems wrong, it never is. Nothing is ever wrong.

Where everything is coming from, every single phenomenal experience, is the beauty of the Self that you are seeking. That Self lives *now*, in the feeling of who you are, not in the feelings that arise in the reference point called "the body."

Movement toward freedom is about receiving the grace of this moment—which is not about anything in particular, but rather noticing from where all the particulars arise. It is about feeling into the love that is offered, while at times, from the mind's perspective, there is the appearance of challenge.

Vigilance must get to a point where it is constant, which, for most, requires that the life be slowed down. There needs to be time to just stop, so that the gift of mind can be received as the tool that it is: simply an indicator of where your attention is. This gift can be received when the mind is watched instead of being seduced by it. And the role of the world is to bring up every latent tendency inside an individual.

Everything is under a perfect and benevolent guidance, and the seeing of this guidance brings unspeakable grace. Ultimately, as you get used to receiving the mind as opposed to being identified with it, the mind's perspective on things becomes meaningless. Its nature shifts from ruthlessness to kindness, and the taste of constant change shifts to the taste of what is changeless. As the chaos melts and the recognition of true stability and beauty becomes self-evident, the organization and wisdom in what seemed to be chaos reveals itself.

Slowing down enough to notice where thought is arising from is a life of clarity, of freedom. In the face of every human challenge, there is the realization that nothing has ever been out of place; nothing has ever been wrong. Everything that ever seemed off at any time replays itself in order for you to discover from where it is coming, which is your *home.* You eventually recognize that divine guidance is orienting everything for the discovery of the untouched essence, the beauty that you are—this Love which is all there is and all there has ever been.

The work is in the vigilance. Vigilance is *now. Now* is eternal. The more intense the mind's story about some situation that it does not like, the greater the amount of vigilance required to discover the truth. This is the nature of the work. There is nothing else that is ever playing.

In this vigilance you discover, "These thoughts are not my thoughts." They are simply a reflection of the degree of forgetting, manifesting in the particular nature that created the experience of being separate. And the taste of the unity, the beauty, lies in witnessing the mechanics of these thought complexes—while orienting yourself constantly to fall into the source from where they come, as opposed to the content that carries you away.

This is the challenge. This is the opportunity. The nature and timing of the play both emanate from the Wisdom that knows the road home.

The Illusion of Powerlessness

The journey of pure surrender is a movement into the core of your human fragility. At the root, every single human being has an inner belief that "who I am is weak and powerless," and must defend from being overpowered in whatever ways it felt victimized as an infant. And out of that arises protective mechanisms that are constructed by thought. No matter what these are, every ego construct has in common at its root a sense of powerlessness, weakness, a fear of being victimized. All of these are derived from early experiences in life.

If you are open, there gradually arises the recognition that everything is set up to dismantle all protection and to discover the truth about your Self. Then there is the potential to welcome what in the past would have brought up a sense of great discomfort.

Instead of the movement to get rid of turbulence, or to control—which is the adaptive mental response—there is now a willingness to see what this fragility and weakness really is. And if one is committed, it will present itself in dramatic or subtle ways, all rooted in an attempt to shield you from the fundamental belief that you are capable of being overpowered. When surrender is true, this is the invitation in.

This journey requires everything because conditioning is so sophisticated. The resultant discovery is the answer to everything that has been searched for. It is the release of protection for someone who is never found. The ultimate discovery is the dissolution of the myth of powerlessness and the falling in love with the Beloved. And the doorway is constantly being offered in multiple ways throughout any typical day.

When you are ready, there is a hunger to just receive and remain still. This runs in opposition to everything conditioned, to open oneself to that sense of powerlessness, and to welcome whatever is happening, exploring what is really in there that can be overpowered. What is really there? Until this exploration is complete, you cannot fully know your Self; you cannot completely embody what is vulnerable to absolutely nothing.

The ego, throughout a normal day, is always subtly positioning itself to be seen, heard, honored, recognized, to look strong, to look knowledgeable. So the opportunity arises for it to get nothing that it is looking for. What will it do if it gets what it is trying to avoid? What will happen then?

And then just open, and look inside and see. This is in direct opposition to what has been conditioned. It is the use of the play and of mental conditioning to disassemble the mind—for mind is just a protective mechanism to get away from a fundamental belief of powerlessness. When these control mechanisms are released, the frequent sense of threat that occurs in life is recognized and felt. And it becomes the doorway into true self-discovery, into meeting what never has been met.

Every thought that revolves around "me," with the exception of some functional thoughts, is generated from this. The issue becomes the doorway, surrender becomes the vehicle, and the beauty begins to flower in everything. Trust begins to overpower every mental response and the sense of someone disappears into no one. The sense of powerlessness vanishes but not into a sense of power: both polar opposites of powerlessness and power dissolve. There remains just the taste of what is.

This is the lover's journey. When there is a grounding in this, the mind's issues and fears become your passion, not your problem.

The Magic Ingredient

I would like to offer what in my experience has been the magic ingredient that transforms the experience of suffering into the taste of grace. We all start out on this journey with amnesia that is built upon our own personal gratification. But something begins to happen when you wake out of your slumber. And that is the remembrance of the beauty from where all of this has come, and of the devotion that is felt for this beauty.

Then there begins the process of wearing down the amnesia, which is all about falling into a deeper calling. This is the beauty of pure devotion. You begin to see that everything the mind saw as wrong is in fact the reason why you are here.

The conditioned egoic perspective is to try to change or get rid of issues with a story that they are sabotaging "my personal well-being." But as there is willingness to be still, and your relationship with your Self deepens, what had been forgotten becomes more alive, and there is a deeper seeing of the benevolence and beauty from where all of it comes. You realize that what the mind hates is actually your purpose, and that your purpose arises out of devotion: devotion to the Beloved, to all humanity.

It is not possible to change the mechanics of the mind's interpretations, though they do slowly morph. The lover's battlefield is simply the willingness to not run from the mind's resistances, fears, judgments, whatever it is that the mind is afraid of. It is being the unmoving space of benevolence that in truth you are. In this, you recognize that you came here for this very reason.

The problem is not the problem—it is the purpose. This is the magic ingredient. When you discover the purpose, you discover love for the role of being a true servant in this play of time and form. There begins to be a passionate relationship with the beauty of receiving what conditioning has conditioned itself to fear. And then the love that is animating all of it is felt. The unity that is animating the appearance of separation, the appearance of conflict, is felt.

It is not about a resolution being needed. It is about seeing that because of the love of everything, in your purity, this has been your heartfelt mission: to hold humanity in the heart of divinity. And then what was misery is discovered to be passion. The light of the Self begins permeating through the hypnosis.

The deeper the realization, the more the suffering of humanity comes down the pike. It does not get smaller; it grows. But what does get smaller until it evaporates is the suffering. And the beauty of the nature of who you are becomes the flavor. Whatever problem your mind might think it has, in fact, is the offering that you have come here to be the humble, loving servant to receive.

The appearance of the problem is, in truth, the resolution. When the mind is blaming, if there is identification with it, it is just the reflection of something that hasn't ripened. You see that something is still asleep and is creating its own misery because it was born out of only feeling "me" and "my wants." But you are so much bigger—so much bigger than the mind can even begin to imagine.

One

Ultimately, one becomes a prostration
to all of it

What was once known
is left knowing nothing

What was once firm
becomes so soft
it becomes almost unrecognizable

What was once you
becomes something
that cannot be defined

But it knows one thing:
it knows love for everything
as its own Self

The Myth of Vulnerability

All of the ego's armor is an attempt to prevent the feeling of vulnerability, no matter what the particulars are. The ego is terrified of feeling any sense of threat. And the subliminal or overt message is that threat or vulnerability is weakening and can injure you. All of the pain and suffering that arises when there is any sense of threat is because the ego is constantly trying to ward it off, deny it, rationalize it, blame something, shield the taste of it. But I would like to explore what the truth of vulnerability is.

What is called "vulnerability" is, for most, momentary times in your life's dream when something causes the protective armoring, which has been called "you," to be torn open. But when trust roots itself enough, what is discovered is that this supposed vulnerability that arises when egoic armor is ripped away is what has blocked you from feeling your own heart all along.

When you are not lost in the ego's attempt to immediately rebuild the shield, and you remain open in it, the taste of vulnerability is the taste of pure love. It is the taste of your own unguarded heart. It is so real. It is so exquisite. The irony is that when you really discover vulnerability, it's no longer vulnerability. Because what makes it painful is not the ripping away of the armor, it's the conditioned mind's immediate interpretation of it as a horror.

From very young life, everyone experiences the mind's interpretation of this so-called horror. And it spins its wheels trying to do everything but revisit that, and this brings up a sense of enormous vulnerability. But it is not really vulnerability that you taste; it's the armor around the story. When trust is rooted and the play tears the armor away, what is discovered is that you love it. It is not weakness; it is true strength that nothing can touch.

You truly cannot be injured; you can only have your conditioning torn apart.

When you discover the truth of things, there is no longer anything in the world to fear. And if fear comes up, underneath it is this luscious, open heart that the mind calls "vulnerable." It is only in being open to the unknown, without control, that you find God. If everything feels neat and familiar and protected, then the armoring is running the show. To the mind's shock, when the construct is blown wide open, the taste of God permeates even the most profane acts.

You know, before I had eyes to see, I could not understand how the actions that occurred in Tibet could have happened, how beings so devoted to kindness could be tortured and torn apart. But I was seeing through the mind, which means I couldn't see. In Taoism, and really in all mystical teachings, it is written that God is found in the darkness. It's not that God does not exist in the light, but it is in the darkness that your mind's eye is shut, out of fear of meeting your own vulnerability. And embracing your own vulnerability is the inroad into true sight, into your own heart, without the conditioned protective armor. You are stripped of knowing anything, not even one concept.

It is such an amazing point when one begins falling in love with the sense of personal vulnerability. It is the beginning of true strength—not strength that is dependent on something, but true strength that is untouched by anything. And what is untouched by anything? Love.

So what is the offering here? You do not have to go very far to realize that life, on a very regular basis, brings up what you call "challenges." But if you forgo the interpretation and you dive into the vulnerability that lies underneath, then you discover the gateway.

In this blessed journey into self-discovery, into what is free of everything, there is meeting what is called "vulnerability" in deeper and deeper ways. This means that the protection slowly begins to fall away. And when it is happening in an environment that is reproducing the memory of pain, there is the experience of what is called vulnerability. This happens more as the shielding melts and the process accelerates. And at a certain point, it no longer feels vulnerable. It no longer feels weakened. What it feels like is absolute freedom, a coming home to your awakening heart.

Everything you could ever possibly hope for lives inside of you. When you are reconciled within, there is nothing in the external play that can cause distress.

You cannot free yourself from what you can't see. What you are conditioned to push away and not look at is reflected back to you in what is called "the outside environment." This is seen by mind as the hell of life, but it is a perfect reflection of the distortions that caused all the armoring that separated you from pure eternal bliss.

While it is absolutely simple, a journey like this is the most challenging way possible to spend a human life. It involves welcoming everything that has been conditioned in the mind to look unsafe. It requires the release of every control mechanism that was a means of survival. This protection only serves to protect a myth, and something recognizes it. This is the way the myth can truly be set free.

When the heart is purified, it is the end of ever experiencing anything as wrong. Nothing is coming out of punishment, but in truth is arising out of grace. This grace purifies the heart until there is a recognition that every single thing is for you, whether your mind can understand it or not. Thus, there is never a need to alter anything.

Working with Vasanas

Egoic issues are referred to in Sanskrit as *vasanas,* and every vasana repeats itself. As the readiness deepens, these issues arise with greater intensity. When you learn how to be with this, the freeing process becomes more rapid. There are gaps when vasanas are not arising. So the mind builds this desire system around the experience that occurs when they are not presenting themselves. That's when everything feels so good because the mind is not active.

But the deepest work is using vasanas as fuel to free you, which is what they are intended to do. The key is to be ready. Instead of wanting to experience life in the absence of the arising of vasanas—which is the way it works for most people—it is to be ready. Simply recognize that this is the active part of what frees you.

It is like doing a workout program. If you are pushing yourself, it may feel challenging. And then when you are done, you feel relaxed. But it is the exercise program that is strengthening you, not the relaxation that is experienced afterwards. This is the same with vasanas. So the key is to be ready instead of frightened.

With experience, everyone recognizes that their particular va-sanas are crystal-clear, obvious, and repetitive. So, at first, when nothing challenging is arising, simply carry the constant intention to rest in the heart. Be with what is unchanging. Feel the silence that lives within so that you are not lost in the habit of identification.

And then when something arises, notice how the mind reacts and the immediate mechanical response. Whether it is physical discomfort in the body, emotion arising out of silence, or uninvited thoughts—just be ready to watch it. This is the doorway into your freedom, as opposed to a problem, which is the way mind interprets it.

Realize that that which is watching is unaffected. The feeling of that which is watching is the feeling of your existence, your being, your heart. Don't try to get away from anything. Just watch the process and feel into what is watching, which is your nature. And then notice the arising of the same habitual dynamics.

For every player, vasanas work in the same manner: there is always conditioned mental resistance. The mind speaks a story of something wrong. But there is no need to change anything. It is about watching the process, which cannot be changed. The more there is effort to do something, the more you get sucked into the illusion. Just watch. Whenever possible, feel what is watching, which is the Self, which is untouched. When it is not possible, simply notice.

When the vasanas arise strongly, I guarantee you that every mind will respond with, "This is so intense. This is too much." Every player. There is nothing unique about it. But when you are ready, notice the mechanical thoughts, which have no inherent meaning.

It is like watching a movie. If you get sucked into it, then surrender your efforts. Trying to get away is fueled by the fear of ego. This is holy burning. This is the intense phase—but it is burning you free. Once there is surrender to the burning, there will return the ability to just watch the movie.

The attention turns to the mind's response, as opposed to the stimulus that is setting the mind off. The stimulus is meaningless. It is the mind's response that creates the experience. So you watch the mind resist. You watch the mind say, "I don't like this." You watch the mind say, "I am failing." You watch the mind say, "I can't handle this."

In the watching comes a separation from the illusion that this has any life in it. And the fuel that drives reactivity begins to weaken. The draw to be sucked in also begins to weaken. Fear begins to fall away. You realize that the thought, "It is too much," is just a façade. It was programmed from the beginning. So it returns, mechanically, as it began. Only now that you have learned how to be with it, it begins to unravel itself. You are not identified, but aware. Be ready. Everything is the gift of grace.

Being ready is being present *now.* You become keenly familiar and welcoming of the mind's story, that it is too much, until you recognize it is nothing but smoke—another thought in an arsenal that is purely mechanical.

What Is Is What You Want

When concept falls away and there begins to be the direct revelation that every single thing that comes forth is directly arising out of the Beloved, there is the very clear seeing that you can always know what it is you want most, because it is always what is happening. And there is the falling away of any interest in what the story of "a future" might bring forth because it would ruin the surprise.

So if there is the appearance of fear or pain or busy mind, there is this revelation: it is the Self in drag. It is what you are seeking. It does not matter what it is. What begins to become the taste— not the concept, but the taste—is *it is what you want.* And to try to plan for what you think you want just messes everything up. And if that appears, there is the recognition that it is arising out of the Self. There is no owner. It is all grace. And you are completely empty, just waiting to receive the grace, having absolutely no interest in what it might mean. Just the receiving is more than enough.

And what is discovered is that what made the aspects that you hated seem so challenging had nothing to do with the offer. It had everything to do with the conditioning. And even the conditioning is ultimately revealed when it appears to be what you want. Because there is the very clear revelation that nothing was ever "mine" to begin with, anyway. I am the receptacle. It is the Master that is the creator.

On the one hand, there is no sense of wanting anything; on the other hand, as soon as something appears there is this recognition: it is *that* that I want. And you always get what you want. The conditioned fear machine is built around safeguarding its perspective of the future. And all that this does is rob you of the grace of the offer.

But when you are ready, you are going nowhere. The running has ended. You are no longer driven by conditioned habits, running on a treadmill and going nowhere. You are empty, full of trust, open to receive. And then grace pours forth like monsoon rains.

Offering Up the Person to Thy Will

What is called "personal volition" or "will" is actually the façade that drives all of the suffering. From the egoic perspective, giving over personal will is the biggest sacrifice and brings up the greatest possible sense of vulnerability. But in actuality, it is completely contrary to this.

Imagine the feeling of releasing involvement with all choice, releasing the sense of burden with all decision-making, being free to fall into the feeling of who you are, of what is untouched, this feeling of pure bliss. Everything peripheral is no longer anyone's responsibility. It is all offered. And in this, something deep inside already knows it is not a sacrifice or an entering into chaos; it is a being carried. This cannot be known by conditioned mind—but something within you knows.

Life transforms from a theme of effort to the feeling of being carried in the womb, in the belly of the Divine Mother, and the fluid in the womb is pure nurturance, it is pure love. What involvement does the fetus have with the mother's choices? It is bathed in the womb of eternal love, in the feeling of I. It is free to fall into it, and all of the appearance of choosing that seems so necessary is just handed over.

A very interesting thing happens when this occurs. It is not only that the burden of the appearance of choice is freed, but the burden of identification with this body is also freed. At this point there is a feeling of falling into from where this dream originally sprang. And then it is just Thy will, unencumbered. It is now God's dream and no longer the dream of personal karma.

For most, this is experienced as a process. There are intermittent tastes of great beauty and then the arising once again of conditioned desire. And each time it comes up, instead of getting caught in the usual trap, there is the opportunity of offering it up as Thy will and falling back into the feeling of I, the feeling of your own essence.

Fear will also arise, fear and desire being the two forces that drive thought. But it works the same way. It appears, and then there is the offering it up and falling back into the womb of pure light. And the miracle is that everything gets taken care of—so much more beautifully, directly, cleanly, than ever before, free of the burden of someone.

The nature of this dream is that it will offer the conditioned mind all of its latent fears and desires, and each time they are offered back, the nectar reveals itself in a more alive way. And the illusion of something separate actually happening "out there" is revealed more vividly.

Bodily issues and worldly issues cease to be yours. It is not that they stop appearing, but they are no longer yours. It has all been offered back to the Source that knows exactly what to do. The mind's terror of giving up "my will" is discovered to be the doorway into eternal bliss.

It is All Only God

The nature of conditioned mind is that it creates an illusory fantasy story about what is God and what is not God, and it perpetuates the craving machinery. In receiving the totality of God's offering, in receiving whatever is up—this is divine connection. Even the feeling of disconnection is connection. The feeling of being lost is being found.

The wearing away of preference arises out of the wisdom that creates everything that is experienced. So the particular experience, whether the mind calls it "pleasure" or "pain," "connection" or "disconnection," is completely irrelevant. What is totally relevant is whether the offer is received.

The nature of the phenomenal play lies in releasing the conditioned habit of seeking. And this is accomplished by these oscillations of what conditioned mind says is God and is not God, is connected and is not connected, is bound and is free. What *is* is God. It is all only God.

Anger

Q: *How do you allow yourself to express anger without identifying with it?*

A: When the heart is open, what the mind defines as anger is recognized to be passion. Passion can be very intense, but it is connective, not defensive. Sometimes, in order to access that, there needs to be the courage to simply allow the body's actions and behaviors to break out of their confinement, out of the box.

But the truth of anger is that it is a protected, defended attempt to connect. If there is the meeting of those defended, protected parts, and the embrace of the vulnerability underneath, then anger is no longer necessary. Instead it becomes an intense expression of passion, and the heart is open. There is no longer a sense of being separate.

It all hinges on the willingness to meet what this conditioned anger is protecting you from.

Physical Pain

Q: *I'm a wimp when it comes to physical pain. Can you help me with that?*

A: Physical pain is no different than emotional pain. It is an aspect of yourself that is hurting and crying out for love. You know very well how to offer love to emotional pain. In fact, physical pain is the by-product of stored-up emotional pain. It is just about being the love that you have discovered you are to something that is hurting.

And there is a secret: pain is only pain when you are separated from it by the mind. The very definition of pain separates you from the experience. You can only know the experience when you are in direct relationship with it. You can only be in direct relationship with it when you are not separate from it.

When you are not separate, you discover something very different. The first phase is just opening your heart to the experience of pain. Then, when there is the feeling of tenderness, the opportunity is to go in deeper with all mental interpretation stripped. And then see what you discover.

When you first meet it with tenderness, then the going in is not disguised as trying to get rid of, which never works. But it is arising out of the love in your heart. Like a scientist with an open heart, just feel into what this is that your mind has called "pain."

Immediately there is a connection with the tenderness. All pain, whether it is physical or emotional, is rooted in an assumption that love is absent. Then what occurs is the recognition that you are the love itself—which opens the door into the mind-blowing realization that it was always only the Self. It was always only pure love all along.

Suffering does not want to be out of suffering. It wants to be acknowledged. It wants to be recognized as justified. What suffering calls "love" is someone who will say, "Oh, I understand. It is so hard." And then suffering can spread. It does not want happiness.

It is not someone's fault—it is the nature of suffering. Your desire for happiness must be greater than suffering's force to survive and thrive.

Bodily Attention

A very helpful teaching and self-reminding is about the habit of how much attention goes into trying to make the body comfortable—how much attention goes into the body. For most, there is a constant and habitual self-monitoring, self-referencing. But as the inner world starts becoming alive, the experience of the outer world starts to disassemble. And by the outer world, I mean the mind's definition of body.

When there is connection with the inner world, there is no relationship with the body. There is relationship with the heart, which is not perceptive but is nectar, pure bliss. And then there is the habit of distraction. What keeps the habit of distraction alive is the attention it is given. So it is not about fighting anything; it is just about noticing.

When there is no attention placed anywhere and the habit of attention comes to rest—when what is felt is felt the same everywhere—there is never a body that can be found. The body only appears when attention falls into a particular location. But when conditioning is not at play and no *attempting* is occurring, then the attention is nowhere in particular and the feeling is equally everywhere.

Don't follow anything. Just notice the feeling of what is not in a particular place. It is so simple. There is no future in it. There is no past in it. Thus there is no character in it. It is like being in dreamless sleep, except you are totally awake. Allow whatever arises to just arise—arise and pass away, while the attention is nowhere in particular but in the feeling that is without definition.

Innocence

Every single thing is filled with innocence. When there appears in the mind's eye a villain—whether the villain is threatening nuclear war or praising the Nazi party; whether the villain is your parent or your job—the villain is actually the mind itself.

No conflict is ever new. Every conflict comes up for your benefit so that you can see from where it is coming and recognize that there is no individual to blame. It is all arising out of consciousness.

There is nowhere God is not, so that which is conscious bears witness to that which has been unconscious action. In other words, that which has been unconscious becomes conscious. Darkness becomes light, because one recognizes that there was really never darkness; all along, it was only the Self. Then the work has been done.

Instead of hiding the habit of doing, which is filled with the fear of survival, you have done your work by remaining still and simply receiving the grace.

The Fantasy of Decision-Making

Perhaps the greatest distraction in this journey for the serious seeker is the illusion of making decisions. For most of you, during the average day, there is a continual experience of choosing. It is the way that the illusion of a chooser, a doer, continues to survive.

True choice lies in intention only, not outcome—the intention to see what is real, as opposed to following conditioned mind, which tells you there are all kinds of choices. But when the intention is to see where choice appears from, you discover that both choice and the chooser are pure myth. It is like a water molecule that is running down a major river that breaks into smaller and smaller tributaries, moves over boulders and smooth regions, goes over waterfalls and flat areas, and this particular molecule of water experiences the process as its own choice.

Take the simplest things that seem like you are making a decision: "Do I feel like taking a walk? Should I clean the kitchen now?" It's all illusion. It is happening by itself. It is never possible to find where it's coming from; and if there is the looking, it is never possible to find where the looking is coming from. There is no individual one who has ever made an individual choice. It is all a smokescreen.

What occurs is spontaneous thought, which carries a subtle message that you are the thinker. With investigation what is found is that there is no "you," no thinker, and thus no decision to make. It's not about making the right choice; instead it's about finding whom the supposed chooser is. The possibility is to be freed from the illusion of decision-making, as if something could be other than it is at any time.

Right now, experience a moment of freeing the habit of involvement with decisions. What occurs is that the juice that drives a future moment is released. Striving to awaken is released. You recognize that there is no choice. It is all being carried, just like the molecule of water.

The very word "decision," inherent in itself, is pure fantasy. There is no such thing as decision. The only choice is in the intention: the humble, open, yielding intention to know your Self. This is never an action. It is not a doing—it's a seeing.

The truth is it is all choiceless. There are not a million possibilities; there is only one. And even that is not quite accurate. There is only *this*. It could not be more simple. It has nothing to do with the appearance of choice no longer appearing. Appearance of choice is pre-contrived. It is what makes the dream seem real. It is what makes "someone" seem real.

The most amazing thing occurs in aligning oneself with choiceless freedom—unchanging, eternal, pure peace. The body does all the same things. It takes care of its tasks. You discover that there was never any involvement to begin with. Your awareness just became contracted and created the appearance of someone with problems to solve. There is freedom from the need to follow thinking. Identification with thought, personal relationship with thought, is unnecessary.

The answer is *now*: it is always now; it is only now. What decision does *now* make? Is *now* making choices? When the attention is on *now*, does the body stop breathing, does the heart stop beating? There is something governing all of it. When the attention is freed, pure divinity carries the whole show. All supposed individual choice is ultimately discovered to be preordained. And devotion to the Ordainer becomes devotion to every single phenomenal appearance.

Let Go of Knowing

What the mind doesn't like

is the greatest grace
the greatest honor

the biggest challenge
of the life

Your mission:
to hold humanity
in the heart
of divinity

It is such a miracle
to see
that all suffering
is optional

What an unbelievable release
of a burden
to let go

of knowing something

and to dance free
like a child

III.

Embracing the
Spiritual Warrior

True Love does not Run

In an effort to get away from what is perceived as discomfort, some individuals have the capacity to break free from the mind and access a taste of great space. When release from the mind's turbulence happens through this route, however, something is lost. Something is gained, but something is lost. What is lost is a discovery that can only arise when there is willingness to face what the ego has built to get away from. True love does not run. True love does not move. It receives absolutely everything as exactly the same.

In the willingness to meet what arises, there is sometimes the experience of enormous burning. This is why this particular path does not appeal to many. In my experience, you cannot fully know the depth of who you are until there is readiness to receive whatever is offered, no matter what the ego's response is.

In the teachings of Taoism, it states that the Tao, or "the way to God," is found in the darkness. It is through the closed door that the opportunity lives. In true surrender, this wisdom brings up everything that you have not seen fully. In the beginning it can cause great fear and intensity, but when this is met, something burns away, and with the burning, you feel everything more deeply. Prior to this, the ability to feel is not as great. Each time the burning happens the experience of feeling intensifies. The totality of everything is felt more acutely because the numbing shell called "ego" is burning away.

At a certain point it becomes clear that this is the ripening process. The sense of trust roots itself so firmly that the mind's fears become your invitation. When this occurs, something that you were previously unable to see begins to reveal itself. Each time a wave of intensity passes, the taste of passion blooms. There begins to be a relationship of pure passion with everything that arises. And the love that is generating everything reveals itself in the willingness to receive the offer.

What ripens the soul is the readiness to receive; and until every single thing is tasted as it is, more ripening is still waiting. If the taste is not oozing with true passion, something is still incomplete. This passion arises out of the taste of love, which arises out of the burning away of what has separated you from feeling everything, from opening to everything, and from moving away from nothing. When this is rooted, where is there to go?

Non-duality is recognizing that the divine exists equally in every single expression. When the mind's impulse to run no longer holds one ounce of sway for you, then you are ready for self-inquiry. Then you are ready to discover from where all expression arises. Then it is time to dive into your true Self.

When the Unconscious Becomes Conscious

The great challenge, the great opportunity, and the unspeakable gift all lie in bringing conscious awareness to what has been unconscious. The root of what is unconscious lies in the belief of a separate doer, a chooser, one who is responsible. And the nature of the journey is going deeper and deeper into this until pure conscious awareness is brought to what has been unconscious. Then it is discovered that there is only the Self, only God, only innocence. It is all pure.

At the root of what is unconscious is a deeply defended belief that "there is something wrong within me." And from the grace of true wisdom, dynamics will replicate solely for the possibility of bringing conscious awareness to what is not conscious and seeing that it has always been only God. What would seem to be good, bad, right, wrong, evil, or not evil, is all equally unfolding on the stage where God plays out karma. Karma is simply holding the unconscious belief that one is separate. This belief is freed when conscious awareness is brought to it.

The last place that this happens, the area of greatest resistance, lies in the beliefs about "myself." It is arrogance, not humility, which holds onto beliefs that something is wrong. True wisdom will cycle those dynamics round and round until there is the absolute revelation that there is nothing but consciousness—there is nothing but God. All actions are under the guidance of that which is completely pure.

When you discover the Self within you, you discover the Self in every single thing; when you discover the innate innocence in you, you discover the innocence in every single thing. If there remains a place where conscious awareness has not met itself within you, there will be the perpetuation of the experience of something being wrong that will arise in particular situations. Conditioning will fight in every way possible to deflect this meeting. It will report that the reoccurrence of these external environments is the issue, but it is the wisdom of pure love that offers the potential of bringing conscious awareness to what has been unconscious. This is the only thing at play.

There was an incident when a small group of thieves came to Ramana's ashram; they stole some things and physically roughed up Ramana. When the people at the ashram got wind of it, they knew who these individuals were and wanted to retaliate. They were very upset that physical harm was done to their master. Ramana's response was, "If you are eating food and you bite yourself inadvertently, do you then choose to punch yourself in the nose?"

When you discover your Self, you discover your Self equally in every single thing, not more in one thing than another. When you receive the teaching of everything—along with the grace in all of it and when everything is received as it is—it is all discovered to be innocent. Then, what was unconscious is brought to conscious attention, and the work of the sage is done. Once it is complete within you, it is complete.

It is not about avoiding your humanity; it is about discovering that, in truth, your humanity is divinity. This revelation is not what you experience when situations are received unconsciously, originating from beliefs about "me." The journey is in discovering who you are by fully entering into the belief of every problem and staying with it, stripped of the content that only separates you from it, until you can feel into the roots of where belief and action are coming from.

It is true that the actions of some in this play, like Hitler, are unconscious actions. But when conscious attention is brought to these actions, what is seen is that unconscious action is arising out of what is conscious. It is recognized that nothing can be different from anything else, that there is no individual. The experience of the individual is unconscious, but when consciousness brings this experience into the light, one sees that there is no individual. It is like waking up and blaming a character in a dream you had at night. The innocence in everything cannot be seen unless your innocence is seen all the way through. Then all that can be seen is innocence, because that's all there is.

It is so obvious that there were never individual ones making individual choices. There never was a stain; there never was a blemish. There is no place for judgment to arise; there is no one left to judge. It is all consciousness. It is all pure light. It is all the love of the Self.

Remain

Bring conscious awareness
to what is unconscious

Remain with the internal
mechanistic responses
all forms of deflection

Remain until
there is the recognition
first of the purity

and second
that it is all arising
out of God

Remain until it is seen
that reality is pure

that there has never
been a stain on the feeling
of your Being

When this is complete
it is the end of suffering

Releasing the Amnesia

Simply feel the beauty. It is your innate nature. When you came into this mortal dream, you took on amnesia. This amnesia has created an almost constant struggle, a struggle in which you are always searching for something. So long as there is identification with supposed problems and issues, there is still grace-filled work waiting to happen. A humbling is waiting to happen.

The nectar lies in what is: that which *is,* whether it's lost in experience or absorbed into the sublime. *What is* is reality. Reality is God. Reality, or God, can be found in the phase of burning away suffering, or it can be found in the phase of celebrating the revelation of your own beauty. All is equally grace. If it is not yet tasted as grace, be assured that taste is inevitable.

As the trust and recognition of what is going on deepens, the running mechanism begins to slow down. There emerges a humility that is ready to receive even the most uncomfortable phenomena. When there is humility, you recognize something very right, even when the conditioned mind is saying it is very wrong. If this is not the case, you are identifying with the mind's story. But that is actually not a problem; it is just part of a natural evolution. The identification is simply reflecting back your level of conscious awareness.

Unwavering Vigilance

We have talked a lot about the process of yielding, receiving, and relaxing, all of which are part of the path of surrender, or devotion. Devotion is the willingness and readiness to receive whatever is being offered. Today I would like to speak a little bit about the other end of this readiness, which is of equal importance. That is vigilance. Vigilance is a one-pointed intention not to follow the mind, not to follow emotions, not to follow anything—but instead, to remain present.

One flavor of vigilance is complete openness, complete softness. The other is a one-pointed fierceness of heart—a one-pointed intention to not yield to the mind. True yielding is yielding to the Beloved. When I say, "not yielding," I mean not yielding to the forces of desire and fear, both of which pull the attention away and create all of the mess. Not yielding is an unwillingness to be weak. Weakness arises in the form of the victim, which is inherent in the root of every ego.

Vigilance is an unwillingness to be consumed by conditioned habit, no matter what arises. It is a recognition that "nothing can overtake me." Vigilance is inherent in everyone because it is an aspect of the Self. You do not have to search for it; it is alive within you. All that is necessary is this vigilance: the refusal to tolerate weakness, the refusal to tolerate the illusory victim—a persona that is nothing more than an imprinted story, anyway. Vigilance is holding on to your Self, which is not moving towards or away from anything.

When the seduction of movement comes to rest, when the vigilance is rooted in the nature of your Self, which is unmoving, then it is time to look and see: *Who am I? Who am I really?* Diving deep within requires no fabrication of a story, but rather it stands on its own, eternally present within your Self.

Whenever there is the feeling of being victimized, it is the Beloved reflecting strength within the vigilance that is waiting to be tapped into. What is required here is a one-pointedness that will not be overcome. Perhaps there will be the experience of being overcome for a period of time, but vigilance will stay with this until the illusion is eventually revealed. Your true nature cannot be overpowered, not by anything.

Remain still as you are, refusing to be seduced, living in the beauty that is alive in this moment, the beauty that is your nature. It is like a ray of Shiva coursing through the center of your being with no ending point. And nothing can alter its trajectory.

So there is the beauty of the path of devotion: the path of yielding, of offering up everything known. There is also the path of vigilance: the path of recognizing the authentic power that lies unmoving within you. Immersed in the Self, the two paths merge into one—both the power and the purity of the Self yielding to itself. Divine feminine and divine masculine meet as one, abolishing the idea of gender, realizing the true nature of the Self.

There is no wavering, for wavering means that you are following a thought. In fact, there is no following of anything. There is only being your Self.

The Spiritual Warrior

The spiritual warrior's battlefield is one of *not* doing. The warrior remains unmoving, existing as a fire. However, there are times when the pull into the experience of being a doer feels overwhelming—like a tsunami flooding in, bringing everything that created the original initiation of the experience of doing. This can be based on events that set off old patterns, or it can be the arising of intensity in the body. It doesn't matter. They are both aspects of mind, and the nature of mind is doer-ship.

The spiritual warrior is that which does not move—not towards, not away from. It cannot be altered. There is a tapping into the one authentic power of the Self. Following the story of "me" is finished. Abandonment is finished. In fact, if the particular dynamics in your life have created a feeling of abandonment, that feeling is a reflection of the abandonment of your Self.

The warrior cannot turn away. Its fire cannot be dampened. Its conviction does not waver. There exists a recognition that something within is larger than anything that appears without. With maturation and readiness, a sense of "Bring it on!" is directed towards everything that conditioning has feared. There is the readiness to see what is real and a fierceness that is unwilling to compromise, no matter what.

The spiritual warrior lives within you. It is the light of Lord Shiva. When there is truly the discovery of what cannot turn away, a re-creation of what was originally turned *from* is going to come flooding through. There is now something ready in you, ready to rip through the façade—not through actions, but by no action at all.

The readiness to see all the way through the illusion of "someone" will not manifest fully until the warrior is discovered, until the recognition that true beauty cannot leave you. The life of the body can be taken; emotions, sensations, and thoughts can be given and taken at any time, while the warrior remains unmoving.

Instead of running from the conditioned ego's discomfort, the warrior creates a stillness that lives within you, ready to see through all of it. If emotion comes up, you remain unmoving, for anything that is changing has no relationship with what is still. What is discovered is that there never has been an enemy. All along, the demon was just a story against which conditioning was trying to protect you.

Be still. Don't be seduced into what is fleeting. If you are concerned about your health, the survival of the body, or the viability of your life, you have not yet recognized the warrior. If you are concerned about anything, you have not recognized the warrior. Even so, the warrior lives within you. It is a power that is alive now.

Submission of the Ego

When you identify yourself as the ego, the word "submission" will cause a contraction, a sense of turning over your power. But in the process of ripening, you begin to discover that it is identification with the ego that actually creates the misery. In the absence of identification, there is only love and beauty and merging. There is everything that was ever sought, and it has always been there. The experience of struggle is created only through identification with the ego.

As identification with the ego begins to loosen with the willingness to do the work, the more mature phase of this process of movement into your Self brings the realization that there is not just the willingness to submit. There is now a hunger for the submission of the ego.

As you begin to taste the beauty more deeply—as well as this aliveness that is unbound, this light of pure love that is in love with itself, manifesting as everything—there comes a readiness and a hunger to offer up what has created the experience of all of the issues. This readiness opposes the ingrained habit of following the ego's beliefs about what it needs and what it fears. It opposes the habit of controlling life by chasing after "what I need" and keeping away from "what I fear." There appears a genuine hunger to offer up the conditioned mechanics that have created the experience of someone separate.

What once was believed to be "you" becomes an offering, a letting go. And in this offering up of the separate one, the beauty that was always sought is discovered. However, if the beauty is sought while coming from conditioned desire, the beauty remains elusive. But when the offering is pure, when all the habits that fed the false notion of "me" are offered to the unknown, then you discover that which you have always searched for and what has always been alive.

You are not giving away your power; you are giving away your misery. It is not the loss of anything, but the recognition of authentic power. It is not about attaining something; it is about releasing, submitting, offering. The concept of "me," which has led to the experience of "me," is wholeheartedly offered. With this offering comes the natural readiness to release what has historically felt like "me," including all of its perspectives, points of view, and tendencies. It is the release of everything known.

Then what is revealed is not only that this beauty has always been alive within you, but that it is so much more. Now the only hunger is to turn the life over, to be freed from the struggles of living from the identification of being "someone."

This is the hunger of true submission. This is when the gates of heaven swing wide open. The individual one cannot walk through those gates because the individual is actually the distraction from recognizing the gates. When there is true purity and the readiness to say goodbye to what has been familiar, you discover that you have never left home. You have never been outside the eternal, untouched nature of your own existence.

As soon as you notice that mind has subtly grabbed onto holy longing, which turns into a desire for "me," consider it a marker to just let it go. As soon as anything arises that the conditioned mind doesn't like, consider it a marker to just receive. Receiving and letting go are not actions. They embody no movement. They are the aliveness in remaining still, remaining as you are—at ease, aware, and truly alive.

The inevitability of being carried by the current of grace can be felt. If it is not felt, that is a reflection that there has not yet been complete and total submission. The second that submission happens, the inevitability is felt.

What incredible grace to live in deep connection with the current that can do nothing but carry you home! Home is reality. Home is your Self. It is the eternal nature of the light of pure divine love that is free of everything, yet simultaneously infuses everything. There is no offering you can make that is large enough to hold the beauty of receiving such a thing.

Getting an Annulment

For the very mature, there comes the realization that freedom, or awakening, is not something that is accomplished by the character. The character is the distraction from that. The character lives in the play of karma, in the mortal dream of separation. As opposed to the character striving to get something for "me," the hunger is to let go of the character, to shift the gaze from a constant diet of the mind's story to the unchanging nature of the heart of being, to what is omnipresent.

There comes a time when you recognize that the beauty comes into expression every time you let go of relationship with the character, with time, with the appearance of phenomena. And there is a turning to the pure light from where all of this comes into manifest expression, to the pure love that is the eternal feeling that lives within but is not bound by anything. There is the recognition that identification with the character is what brings forth all of the trouble. And the moment that identification is freed, there is the taste of what has never known trouble.

The thing is that there is not the readiness to really marry, to unify with the eternal nature of this pure love, until there is the readiness to divorce yourself from relationship with the character. When there is this hunger, there is very deep maturity and readiness. Every time identification with the character arises, as opposed to grabbing onto it and running with it, the hunger is simply to let it go, to relax, to feel the unchanging nature of the heart that is not in relationship with anything but itself. The hunger is to release conditioned habits that bring on the experience of doing, of choosing, and to feel that which is actionless, which is the nature of being.

It is not possible until there is the hunger to divorce yourself from the character, for the character is the obstruction. It is not possible to be ready to divorce yourself from the character until you have tasted the beauty of this light of pure love that is the unchanging nature of your Self. The marriage to this can take place not only after there is divorce from identification with the character but when there is actually an annulment. Then there is gifted the sight of recognizing that the character never really existed. It was just a dream that drew attention, based on sensations, emotions, and thoughts that spun the whole web. The offer of the dream is what is called "karma," the problematic dynamics that continue to reoccur, causing the angst and drive, the desires and fears.

So the first step lies in the recognition that that is not where real satisfaction comes from. And there is a readiness to move on from the relative experience that is a constant rollercoaster. There is the readiness to turn the attention to the unmoving nature of the beauty of your being, which is pure joy, which is everything the character has ever desired, even though the character is the distraction.

So there is this readiness to let go of the character instead of following it. And as this letting-go process begins to occur, what is revealed is that none of that was ever anything more than a daytime dream, which is identical to a dream at night. What is revealed is that your nature has always been untouched, that the beauty is who you are, that the only way identification happens is if the attention is pulled away from the very nature of your existence that is eternally, unchangingly *now*.

And it is felt—not by the body, but everywhere. It is the beauty of the heart and the severing of this hypnosis called "linear time." And it is the taste of the infinite, eternal nature of the pure light of being.

Just feel it; imbibe the nectar that has nothing to do with doing or changing. Just feel the heart. It is so simple, so alive, the centerless feeling of your very existence. True marriage with the Beloved is the annulment of suffering.

Awakening to Death

The ordinary person in the spiritual arena is pursuing enlightenment. However, the one who is in pursuit is the conditioned mind, so then enlightenment turns into a thing to be attained. The ego becomes the pursuer. The only thing that can be pursued is an object, something defined by the mind. So we have the ego as a pursuer of an object it calls "enlightenment."

At the same time, there is what the ego is terrified of—death. At play here, then, is a desire for enlightenment and a fear of death. However, everything is topsy-turvy. The truth of it is actually reversed, the opposite of what is perceived. True enlightenment is what is revealed with egoic death: this brings the death of the pursuer, the death of the reference point, the death of being bound to this body, and finally, the death of the relationship to the appearance of the individual. In truth, this is not death but life.

When the relationship with the egoic mind dies, it does not seem like death, because pure light, pure life, and pure beauty are what remain. In some instances, the beauty immediately reconstitutes itself into something about "me," but this is just a distraction—mechanical and lifeless. The lasting appearance of beauty occurs in moments when the conditioned program relaxes, when the sense of "someone" relaxes completely. What is discovered is that the seeking of egoic death is, in truth, the seeking of life. When there is true readiness to die, what the mind calls enlightenment becomes inevitable.

For most, the primary driver for enlightenment is being enamored by the story of "me and my life," "my future," "my body," and "my circumstances." But the deeper the taste of what is true, the clearer the seeing. The clearer is the seeing, the greater the hunger. Instead of the packaging of some pleasant experience that has been defined by mind as something to attain, what occurs is a hunger for what the mind calls death.

This hunger can only manifest when there has been the direct taste of so-called "death" as the light of God, the light of the Self. So long as there is relationship with striving and the story of "me," there is still a sense of being enamored with the striving one. But that mechanical character is discovered to be that which siphons the life, as opposed to that which *is* life. This is looking directly at the meaning of true death. Compared with this, birth and death of the body are really like child's play.

When you have died in relationship with the separate character, you have died in relationship with the body, with time. There is no one left to be found. Then what is left to die? Herein is the birth of true enlightenment. When this experience goes deep enough, everything reverses. The yearning is no longer about the mind's concept of enlightenment. There is the revelation that what the mind believes to be death is actually life: pure love and happiness, the eternal taste that has always been. Each moment there is the taste of beauty is a moment when relationship with the play of time dies.

In the ripe one, the hunger is taken, dissolved. But before this, the mind works so subtly; it weaves a story, wanting the desire to be taken when it is really being driven by the desire to attain the ultimate pleasure that it calls enlightenment. This is just the habit of being constantly distracted by conditioned desire and fear.

Without the beauty that you are, the beauty that gives life to this flesh and blood, and without the vital energy, this body is nothing more than a corpse. That which gives life to the body is always available because it is your existence. When you fall into the feeling of your existence, you fall into your Self. When you fall into the feeling of your Self, you have let go of the habit of believing a story about who you are. When the story is no longer interesting, when it no longer pulls your attention, it falls away. The habit of living through a reference point falls away. Then the eternal nature of pure bliss reveals itself for what it is and what it has always been.

What is it that has fallen away? You, or the idea of you, has fallen away. Your existence ceases to be *my* life; instead it is just life. This is true life, the life of divinity, the life of unity, the life of pure luminosity: centerless and timeless, it is the simple feeling of your very existence. With this revelation comes the death of distraction, the death of being enamored of "my story." Then a deeper passion is recognized, and this is the passion of all passions.

Being in the World, not of the World

I'd like to speak about what is meant by being "in the world, but not of the world." In the egoic play of separation, what brings forth all of the struggle is living a life that is purely about the relationship of object to object. The fundamental object is the reference point defined by mind as body, or "me." Because the mind perceives all objects as discrete and separate, the body experiences everything else as other separate objects. And anything that is not perceived as an object is perceived as nothing at all.

When the habit of identification is freed, it is the contraction into the reference point that is freed. This contraction is driven by conditioned desire and fear. When there is true humility, as well as the hunger to remain still, the habit of following that which appears to be moving ceases. This is not a doing. It is a surrender, a release.

In the early stages of this process of surrender and release, the experience is typically still coming from the contraction. Eventually, however, the contraction is recognized to be driven by the act of following desire and fear. This following causes conscious awareness to contract into a reference point, an individual "me" who then experiences the world of separation.

The fundamental force that builds all of this is the creation of thought. However, when there is readiness to remain still instead of latching on to each thought as it arises, the thought becomes a reminder to just let go and relax. There begins to be the taste of what is unmoving and what is unaffected. There is the taste of what is without reference, without time, and without an object.

Each time a phenomenon appears that has the potential to grab attention, it offers the possibility to simply receive, to relax. Then the contraction eases, and the unbroken sense of that which is objectless remains.

This feeling is whole and full, totally unstained. It is not that the appearance of objects stops manifesting, but in order for an object to be an object, it must be separate, and in the feeling of this relaxation, you realize that all that appears is appearing within the experience of the oneness of everything. What seem to be objects are recognized to be appearing within the heart of being. They cease to be separate from the feeling of your Self.

With this realization of oneness, you see that no distinction exists between what is called "form" and what is called "formless." You recognize the seamlessness between the two; you can see that what is reflected is unified and whole, pure and untouched. Actually, you recognize you are in everything. And although you are in the world, you are not experiencing separation. You are eternally unmoving.

Instead of perceiving the karmic entrapment of separation, you see that everything that appears to move is the dancing light show of pure divinity. You are everywhere, but you are nowhere the mind can find. You are in everything, even though from the conditioned egoic mind's perspective, you are nothing. Then the dream reflects harmony. It reflects the love that is pure.

This journey is experienced by many as an enormous challenge because the separate reference point defined as "me" is built around survival. However, when there is maturity, there is readiness to let go of this "me"; and as the maturation process unfolds, you discover that your true survival, your true aliveness, is built on letting go of this reference point, a revelation that is the opposite of the "story." Your very survival depends on releasing the habit of distraction that creates the experience of the separate one, and you realize that nothing is worth the compromise. Then you are all but home-free.

Living in the moment, as the moment, eternally unbound in everything, you are unaffected by anything. The moment the habit returns to the reference point, the ante is upped and the sting is intensified. This evolutionary process continues until there is the recognition that "my very survival" is not based on the survival of the character, but rather the release of the character. It is no longer object to object; it is consciousness totally absorbed in itself. It is centerlessness absorbed within itself, pure love absorbed within itself. There is no separate one to be found. The habit of doing evaporates, and the experience becomes something that cannot be spoken but can be tasted in the feeling of your being—the feeling that is without a center but is everywhere. When attention relaxes, that which reveals itself is the heart.

Every time a phenomenon arises, there arises the opportunity to just relax and let it go. This is how stabilization roots itself. This is being *in* the world, but not being *of* the world.

True Resurrection

With every offering that is gifted in this life, Easter Sunday is the day of the resurrection, a symbol for freedom from the ego. Several days before Easter comes Good Friday, the day of the crucifixion, a symbol for the burning away of ego. What is the doorway into resurrection, into the liberation from ego? The doorway into resurrection is the offering up of every thought.

To do this, your life must be slowed enough so that you become present enough to actually offer up every thought. This is not about attempting to prevent a thought from arising; it is simply offering up the thought as soon as it is recognized. You can offer up a thought to the Holy Father, or you can offer it up to wisdom, to benevolence, or to the source from where it comes.

The offering up of thoughts is symbolized not only by the resurrection, but also by the crucifixion because, from the ego's perspective, the offering up of thoughts is offering up the life of the ego. The ego will struggle any way it can to stay alive—it will create a battle. Facing this battle is what is symbolized by the crucifixion.

A crucifixion, however, exists only from the perspective of being identified with the ego, or with "someone" struggling to survive. With one-pointedness, identification will shift from the dying ego to that which is liberated already. This shift in identity is the true resurrection: it is liberation from being bound by time and form. You realize that you have never left Heaven, that being liberated has always been your nature.

There is a freeing from the struggle and suffering of the mortal dream of separation, which is built upon whatever apparent karmic predicament is being offered. When the life is slowed enough, there is the possibility of being fully present—to turning over every thought as it comes. Now you no longer live in the arena of relationship with thought or mind; now you are set free.

This awareness is not something for a select few; it is the nature of everyone's existence. But it is indeed true that in this mortal dream the realization of this awareness is very rare, simply because, from the conditioned ego's perspective, it requires everything. However, you do discover that, in truth, this realization of your awareness is offering everything in return. It is offering true life, eternal life—the nature of your very consciousness, the nature of heart that you really are. This is what is known as Christ Consciousness, as Buddha Mind, as the Self, that which is not bound by location or time. It is what is here *now.*

When thought is offered up as it arises, the centerless, eternal nature of this awareness becomes self-evident. It is felt within the heart, and the heart is the pure bliss of your being. It is neither in the past nor in the future, for past and future exist only when the thought process is not offered up. This is about the nature of reality, and reality is *now.* It is always here *now.*

Now is not in time, just like Heaven is not a place, but it is the nature of your being when you are not identifying with separation—when you have the willingness to allow this ego to be crucified, to be unraveled into nothing. And inherent in the nothing is everything, which means *you* are everything.

You are certainly everything to me!

It is all such a mystery, from where this love comes.
How something so totally impersonal
can taste so overwhelmingly personal.
All that I can say is how it becomes everything.
What happens in the life, what happens in the body,
what occurs based on circumstances—
everything becomes so secondary.

And there is this gratitude with every breath for this
that you cannot describe
but is alive in your heart as a love affair
with something more precious than you can speak.

It calls on you, in you, to you, through you.
And it only grows.

All that once seemed important becomes unimportant.
This love becomes the only thing of importance.
And "importance" is not the right word.
"Passion" is much closer.
But that, too, is far too limited.

It becomes everything, everything good,
everything whole, everything cherished.
All that could be wanted and more.
And it already is.
And it lives in your heart.
And you cannot believe it.

Discovering Your Own Innocence

The recognition of your own innocence is probably the most challenging work. Coming out of the seamless nature of pure heart, the newborn infant feels that "I am everything." When there is conflict, before the adaptive shell crystallizes, the infant believes that he or she is the problem. As she feels this energetic clash, she constructs the belief that "something is wrong with me." The life mission then revolves around trying to make safe what feels inherently unsafe inside.

If your awareness is seamless, you recognize that you are everything. When the human experience of separation is seen through the totality of consciousness, there is the recognition that whenever the separate one sees something wrong out there, that is a deflection of an original absorbed belief that "something is wrong with me." Anything in the world that is brought up that feels other than innocent is pointing to some, perhaps very subtle, level at which you have not met your own innocence.

It is only possible to see "wrong" where aspects of the mind remain—where the pure light of awareness has not shone fully. False beliefs, all of which originate around "myself," have not been liberated. The mind is especially tenacious around its belief in "the story of me." In fact, the greatest tenacity lies with the battle in relationship to that story. Again, the habit of seeing something as unsafe or wrong out there is a deflection. Of course, the grace is that you are pure innocence.

Over time, it becomes clear that thought complexes are conditioned. They do not ask someone's permission; they arise spontaneously based on repetitive stimulation that is always pointing to something that has not been fully recognized.

Distraction tactics attempt to allow this separate character to survive by presenting it with the belief that the dynamics are external. Either "I am screwing up and hurting somebody in the external world," or "someone in the external world is screwing up and hurting me." But this is all in a continuum. You are the center of your life dream.

This process is challenging because held in the nature of conditioning is a belief that "I should change"—the thought and emotional complexes that depict "me" and "who I am" should change. However, whenever there is a sense of being truly present, it is clear that the belief is a protective survival mechanism built against a sense of threat, based on the belief that "something is wrong with me." But you come to discover that the believed threat is not external: the externalization is protection, and the underlying belief about the threat is really that "I am the threat."

The nature of pure love is that it is an open receptacle to every single thing; it is not trying to get away from anything. It is even the receptacle for conditioning. When conditioning is received in connection with the eternally present heart, in which there is no experience of a separate one, there arises clear mind, pure awareness.

When old patterns of misunderstanding arise, awareness will morph into awareness of something *in particular*. This is the birth of mind. But this birth is healing the mind because it sees the mechanical nature of the referencing. Simultaneously, it recognizes the choiceless nature of what perpetuates the experience of separation, and that it is no one's fault. Here lies the birth of compassion, true compassion that sees the innocence. This compassion feels the suffering of the misunderstanding but recognizes the innocence.

When you recognize that every single thing is innocent, there occurs the most unspeakable experience of relaxation. When you see that any time there is the experience of anything that is not innocent, it is bringing up something that has not been seen inside of "me." Then the world becomes a gift of profound teaching. Relationship with wrong and right, good and bad, dissolves into nothingness. Conditioned automatic responses will come up in the mind, but the innocence of those is seen. What was once personal is recognized to be innocent, and what recognizes the innocence *is* the innocence; it is the seamless, unbroken nature of your Self. Then the flavor of the heart shines, the relationship with fear falls away, and what truly cannot be disturbed by anything is revealed to be the nature of who you are.

The mind is intense in wanting karma to resolve itself. The more the numbing wears off, the more there is a yearning to be free of the things that create disturbance. Now it can be recognized that the desire for things to be different lies in the inability to see the innocence of what is already playing.

The environment you often find yourself in is the gift of divine wisdom, which points to subtler and subtler ways in which you have not directly tasted your own purity. When humility is ripe, you discover that there is nothing outside of God. Then you live only in the bliss of love.

Vigilance lives in the intention, not the outcome.
It lives in the moment, not the future.
The intention is humble and comes from the heart.
The intention is to be present, but it is not about an outcome.
Thus, it is not infused by effort.
It recognizes that the outcome is up to a higher wisdom.

What is eventually discovered is that the intention is enough,
that the outcome is experience, and that experiences are changing.
The surrender lives in the intention,
the humble, pure intention to be true.

Vigilance is not about the future; it is not about a goal;
it is not about enlightenment.
It is about the humble intention to be true now,
while seeking nothing.
If there is no seeking in it, there is no doing in it.
It is just a remembering.

The Role of Content

I'd like to speak about the role of content in the experience of life. As many of you have tasted repeatedly, life is like being on a stage, with characters playing out their karma. This life drama offers an invitation because as the nature of the play morphs, you fall more deeply into what is untouched by the play of change, and it becomes more love-infused and light-infused. Sometimes content is pointing to what is contentless, to the beauty that is felt when relationship with mind relaxes.

Content continues to inform, not through the particulars of the content, but through the revelation that it is irrelevant. Its value lies in the recognition that situations that cause reactivity will repeat themselves because roles are driven by the karmic condition. So the situations that set off reactivity will cycle around again and again.

The grace is that you begin to discover that the play has already been written, that it is all just karma repeating itself. The more you see the impersonal nature of what once seemed so personal, the less you get swayed by the flavor of the content and the more you feel into the unchanging nature of what is contentless. That is the pure beauty that unifies everything. And this beauty is pure love.

You begin to recognize that no matter what a character may be saying or doing, when the rehearsal is over, there is only love. You see that the roles are being played to free relationship with content and to recognize the underlying connection with love itself. This is not only the case with what others may say and do, but also with what is called "my own mind." The content repeats itself, but underneath the content is the taste of unity, beauty, and light. The more this is tasted, the more the content begins to reflect that. At times, old dynamics will recycle for the possibility of offering ever-deepening humility—which means letting go of the reactive habits and seeing clearly that we are actors on a stage, playing out the roles of our karma.

Everything is being orchestrated by true wisdom in order to gradually free attention from content, whether it is what is perceived to be another or what is perceived to be "my own mind." As content becomes irrelevant, language morphs into beauty, into wisdom as opposed to thought. Then everything arises out of the love that unifies instead of the karma that created the experience of being separate. The deeper in you go, the stronger the stimulus must be to cause a seduction into identification with the reactive mind. The process is a continual humbling until the sense of someone separate has unraveled itself. Then it is recognized that all along it was content itself that created the experience of separation.

With this recognition, the battle ceases—the battle that creates demands on the mind to perform in a way that reflects that "I'm a good person." You begin to see that the mind is the stage and that the stage is an offering. Grace is offering you the possibility of seeing the mechanical nature of what is actually pure innocence. Then words begin to flow that carry content for others, but not for you. You are no longer in relationship with content; you are in relationship with the love that unifies everything. Tracking content is no longer important. The wisdom that was there prior to conditioning springs forth, a wisdom that is free of knowing.

It's All an Inside Job

When you leave behind the habit of following phenomena and turn the attention inside, something quite astonishing happens. As you become truly rooted inside—not intermittently but continuously—you wonder, with a bit of shock, how this revelation could have ever been missed. You discover that everything that was once experienced as external was internal all along. The entire five-sensory, three-dimensional movie show is all arising from within.

When you connect with what is eternally real, which is eternally now, you see the whole play within the feeling of your very existence. This feeling is not *somewhere;* it is *everywhere.* The feeling is not housed by anything, but everything appears within it. You begin to see that the whole play is an inside job. It's all within you. When this is recognized, not as a concept but as an experience, then identification with any particular aspect of the play is freed. Whether the body is sitting with eyes closed or it is running about, everything that is happening is directly revealed to be internal.

You realize you have never been out of meditation. You see that there is no such thing as externalization. Like a black hole, except that it is all light, nothing can escape this realization. The gravitational force is so strong that attention is pulled completely within. And like a black hole, where it has been mathematically shown that time does not exist, there is no time inside this light. You realize that the experience of without has actually been within all along. What is there to do? There is no one to do anything.

Like a fetus in a womb, where the amniotic fluid is pure light and kindness, the developing fetus is dreaming of time and form, of "my life" from infant to old person, of all the particulars as the life progresses. But all along, this being is bathed in a fluid of pure beauty that contains all the sustenance. This is the mortal dream, and this dream is within you. You are what cannot be experienced in the dream because the dream is experienced within you. The grace lies in the possibility to discover for yourself what reality is.

Every time the habit of following phenomena falls into a localized point of reference, hypnosis has taken root. But every time there is direct investigation into "who I really am"—which, in truth, is reality—the hypnosis is broken. When the hypnosis has been broken deeply and consistently enough, there is nothing else to do but to break free of an addictive habit. It's all a dream. You have never suffered, never struggled, never broken through anything, never deepened. The wisdom that is offered points to the reality that it is all a dream appearing within you. And the beauty is that no matter how compelling the dream it is still all happening within you. What once appeared as form is felt as formless, and within this formless reality, there exists the manifest expression of form.

This dream happens within your own conscious awareness. And in the dream, the mind of the dreamer is within the womb of the Holy Mother, the endless ocean of light and love, within which you are always immersed.

IV.
The Doorway into Your Self

*The beauty and grace of self-inquiry is that it pulls
the habit of attention from the relative play of phenomena
to the absolute, unchanging taste of your Self.*

*When you fall into the question of "Who am I?"
you fall into the subject, you fall into your Self.
When you fall into your Self, you fall into reality.
When you fall into reality, you fall into God.*

What You are Not

The greatest place to begin in extricating yourself from bound-edness lies first in seeing what you are not. This is because the amnesia is a trance, which creates the experience that you are something that, in fact, you are not. So the whole illusion begins with this mental, sensory, emotional complex that says, "I am this body." It's where it all begins.

It is clear that there is something aware of the body or there would be no body awareness. What is aware of the body is the presence that is eternally alive. It is the only thing that is not away from you, not an object that appears based on perceptive experience. So it seems that perhaps the most direct place to begin lies in the recognition of what may seem to be "me," but, in fact, is an object that "I am aware of."

It starts as a *not this* and *not that*. It begins as a recognition that anything that I am aware of, I am not. I am simply aware. I am not limited to or bound by anything I am aware of. So when thought appears: I am not that. Sensation appears: I am not that. Emotion appears: I am aware of but not defined by it. There can be this mainstay of negation around every single object of appearance that appears in a location in time. There can be the recognition, I am simply aware, which is not in location or in time; it is eternally now and it is everywhere.

This orientation of systematically recognizing what does not define "me" breaks the illusory hypnosis by defeating the ap-pearance at its roots. As this becomes natural—which is what will happen if true conviction remains, and conviction super-sedes the conditioned habit of seduction—then the particulars stop mattering. Then all that matters is seeing what you are not, what you are not defined by, what you are not limited by.

Yet you are aware of all of it, eternally present in the unchanging, unbroken flavor of your existence. Every time the habit of falling into a point of reference returns, it is possible to simply recognize, "I am aware of that, not bound by it." It appears and disappears in time but I am timeless awareness, aware of everything that appears and disappears.

As you become freed from the hypnosis, what becomes obvious is that it is not the character that awakens. It is consciousness that awakens to itself out of a hypnosis that "I am defined by a reference point, yet I am aware of all of it." It is so clear, and the awareness that is aware of all of it is untouched by any of it. It is not in past or future; it is now. It is not somewhere; it is everywhere. The moment one touches the phenomenal display of thought, sensation, and emotion, your attention moves away from present consciousness.

Anything that "I am aware of," no matter what it is, you see that "I am not limited by this; I am aware of it." It does not define "me"; in fact, it doesn't define anything. It is just phenomena. The deeper in one goes, the more seductive the perceptive experience must become in order to hold the potential to hypnotize. At the same time, the deeper the knowingness, the stronger the conviction to remain unmoving.

Then arises the perfect timing for the perfect question: "If I am not anything that I am aware of, then who am I?" It is possible to feel into "who I am"—not the character feeling into who I am, but first a recognition that this is an object appearing and I am aware of this, though not defined by it.

In breaking the trance, it is possible to look and see, "Well, then, if I am not an object of appearance, in reality who am I?" The dream ceases to be objectified and is recognized that it is all a phantom of imagination. Then you stand as stillness, the eternal, free nature of being. Then the prison cell of being identified as a point of reference, at a point in time, is liberated—and you taste what has never been touched, what has no past or future. This journey into breaking out of amnesia demands constant attention.

But attention is not effort. Attention is the release of effort. Attention is not someone; it's liberation from the illusion of experiencing someone. It is not in the future. It is in reality, which is timeless, which is *now*.

The beauty is discovered to be what has always been. What is definable is phenomenal. I am aware of phenomena. I am the eternal awareness that is aware of all phenomena that flows through eternal presence that is always now. And the games played by the habit of seduction blow through again and again in the play of time, arising for the appearance of someone. Then there is the self-reminding, "Not this, not that." And then, "Who? If not this, not that, then who am I?" This is the sum total of all of it.

Consciousness conscious of itself—this is what the mind calls "awakening." What impact does the character "me" have on consciousness conscious of itself? There's no intersecting point. Anything I am aware of, I am not. In the rooting of the recognition of what "I am not" is the perfect time to look and see, "Well, then, who am I?"

I am home. I have always been home.

Everything in Perfect Alignment

Inherent in the feeling of silence, stillness, and wholeness—the unchanging feeling of what is always present—is a direct connection with the sense of how right everything is. I do not mean that everything is experienced as right when it is perceived as separate. It is the realization that the feeling of rightness is inherent in the Self and independent of anything that appears to change.

For most, there is a tapping into it when life plays itself in a way that is in direct alignment with their desire system. But what is discovered is that feeling that is so right has nothing to do with what is changing. There is a constant unchanging feeling of the rightness that is inherent in your nature.

You realize, from the mind's perspective, it always seemed to be dependent on the particulars that were playing—but it never was at all. And the true recognition feels so profoundly right, such that you cannot imagine how you could not see it before. When this is tapped into, things that would cause distress arise, but the feeling of how right everything is remains because it is not attached to the movie show.

But it's not because the movie show changes in accordance with the desire system. Instead it is because you begin to be freed from a roller coaster that is dependent on the particular stimulus that is playing in the movie. You discover that the feeling that "all is right" never came from an event to begin with.

Then when the stimulus cycles around that had caused the feeling of wrong—but the habit of retracting into the mind's protection doesn't occur and there is remaining with what is eternally still—that same stimulus brings up a deeper state of rightness than has ever been known before. This is because it is a rightness that is discovering where the feeling of rightness comes from.

Feeling in alignment is dependent only on whether you are aligned with your Self. You recognize that the particulars in the play have in fact always been irrelevant. When you realize this, the most catastrophic occurrence is irrelevant. And what *is* relevant is the eternal nature of alignment, which feels so right.

Then when the feeling arises in the subtlest way that something is not right, it becomes a self-reminding mechanism that "I have been pulled away from my Self." Then the play of the world becomes the instrument to set you free, which it has always been intended to be. Then the uncomfortable symptoms of the body become a reminder to set you free, which they too have always been intended to be.

When you are in alignment, when the unbroken feeling of the rightness of *being* is no longer wavering, when the oscillations of body and world no longer cause any shift in the feeling of the unchanging rightness of your being, this is the time when there is readiness to look and see, "Who am I really?"

Three Steps to Freeing the Mind

I'd like to talk about a daily exercise that—if one is truly committed to it—will break you free from the oscillations of the swing of mind. There are three steps in this exercise.

The first is simply to notice what is noticing this body. As soon as there is observing what is noticing the body, instead of the experience being "the body is who I am," there is an awareness that this form is an object that is appearing. And the subject is what is aware of it.

So immediately what is aware is arising out of still space, as opposed to being governed by conditioned mind. Here you are simply noticing what is aware, what the mind calls "me." Once that feels fairly comfortable and stable—and it will be lost and remembered, lost and remembered—whenever there is the re-membering, simply shift the gaze from inside-out to outside-in, noticing the body, being aware of the body.

When that becomes calm and obvious, the second step is to look for the "I" that the whole story is built around—to allow your awareness to dive deeper in, searching for the "I."

In the beginning, when daily activities are in motion, they will pull attention away. And for most, it is easier when attention is pulled away to take the first step to just notice: to notice the body, notice what is happening, notice what is noticing. And once that roots itself, then look for the "I."

Upon investigation into the "I," the byproduct is always the same: nothing is found. There is the discovery that I cannot find the essence of myself.

126

And then there is the third step: What remains? Simply feel what remains. Life will offer every opportunity possible to distract your attention. This is because you cannot be free unless you are free in the face of everything that has the tendency to distract.

If this tool is used only at times of distress, it will be experienced as extremely difficult. If it is used every time the possibility reveals itself, eventually remembering happens in shorter intervals—it is the nature of it—until it no longer needs active intention. Until it becomes automatic, because it really is just breaking an addiction.

Thus the three steps are

- noticing what is noticing the body from this place of stillness

- looking for the "I"

- feeling what remains

Remembering

It is just about letting go
of the habit
of being seduced

into an illusory one
who needs something
at all cost
at all times

There will be forgetting
and there will be remembering

until the remembering
roots itself deep enough

that you can no longer forget
the remembering

The Only Question is Who?

This teaching boils down to two aspects: one is the welcoming of every single thing, the recognition that every moment is your opportunity—opening your heart, being, and attention to what is. This is the path of surrender. And then there is the path of wisdom: the use of mind as a helpful tool instead of a distraction. If this is taken to heart, the only question that is worthwhile is, "Who?" It does not matter what the initial question may be. Every question is a distraction from the real question. "I need to pay my mortgage." *Who does?* "I feel distressed." *Who?* "I don't like this." *Who?*

After you seriously look at this question, then you can follow any other question. But what you notice is that all other questions fall away because they are a distraction. They are an assumption that is conjured out of the familiar myth of someone.

The opportunity with every single mental activity that arises is to look and see to whom it is occurring. I can tell you the by-product of this: the oscillations of what opens and closes for you eventually become stabilized. The recognition that there is no one in there becomes constant. It is inevitable. Then what happens to all the other questions? What happens to the problems, to "my life," "my future"? What happens to "Why?"

What becomes clear is that other questions are driven almost exclusively by fear. If inquiry is driven by fear, trying to get away from discomfort, it is not true inquiry. If there is fear, just open and receive whatever is. If there is true willingness, the fear will dissolve. Just wait patiently with what is occurring. Whatever appears disappears and is ultimately discovered to touch nothing.

To cut at the root of what builds the entire fabrication, simply ask, "Who?" Never use this to get away from anything, but instead use it to dive into the root of who you are.

The Secret of You

Everything you know about yourself is all just thought. If the habit of following thoughts about "who I am" is released, there is just a childish curiosity arising from a place of complete unknowing. It is not about the need to find out, not about some outcome, but just the joy of a child exploring the unknowingness of "me." Free of goal, free of concept, free of carrying someone who is trying to awaken or discover some *thing*. But just playing, knowing nothing.

When you are looking inward to see, "Who am I?" there is awareness of sensations, feelings, thoughts passing by, ever-changing—and the feeling that I am aware of the arising of them. But what am I? If there were an answer, it would ruin the fun.

And then what is discovered is the mystical secret, the divine mystery. The less it becomes about getting some thing, the more the secret reveals itself. Going after some thing bypasses everything. But in falling in love with the mystery of "me," there is a state of awe. The mind is left in wonder. And the heart comes alive.

Like a child playing hide-and-seek, the joy is not in finding the one hiding. It is in all of it, living out of the mystery. The gaze turned within, without a goal. Just for the sheer joy of it!

And then you discover that the mystery is endless. It is the mystical secret. *You* are the mystical secret.

A Simple Explanation of Self-Inquiry

I would like to speak about the gift of self-inquiry. Most standard forms of meditation involve turning the attention in a one-pointed way to something in particular, some object in particular. This can be very helpful because it helps to tame the habit of the wandering mind so that it becomes more singularly focused.

It is the rare aspirant who matures to a point where what naturally arises is a yearning to look and see who is the one meditating on some particular object. It is turning the attention to the subject of the meditation, instead of to the object. Who is the "I" that thinks and feels and acts?

In the play of subject-object dynamics, the subject, the story of "who I am," is in constant relationship with objects. Instead the possibility is to turn the attention to the subject. It breaks you free of subject-object dynamics into the core from where it all comes.

"Who am I?" Fall into your essence. And then whatever happens to be appearing are all objects that the subject is aware of. Instead of the habit of attention directed toward the objects, it turns to the subject who is aware.

Sensation arises. From where does it come? Whom is it affecting? There is the potential of falling deeper into direct relationship with your Self and farther away from the assumption of someone who is constantly conditioned to track particular objects. Shift the gaze to the subject itself.

In the beginning, there is an inherent immediate relationship with an assumption that "I am experiencing whatever is arising." But as you fall deeper into the direct revelation of what is this "I," the attention falls away from any relationship with subject-object.

So if the body hurts, it is not a question of *what* hurts. The question is, *To whom?* And the attention remains there until there is falling all the way in. When this occurs, the "I am hurting" goes away because there must be a subject to experience an object. When you fall into the subject, you fall into your Self. When you fall into your Self, you fall into reality. When you fall into reality, you fall into God.

The beauty and grace of self-inquiry is that it pulls the habit of attention from the relative play of phenomena to the absolute, unchanging taste of your Self. The key to this is consistency, such that there is a breaking out of living in the superficial realm of cause and effect, of karma, of subject-object dynamics. And a falling deeply into the pure nature of your Self.

Where Am I?

We have spoken a great deal about the illusion of past and future, that it is all imaginary. You have never for an instant existed in a future or a past. What is real is now, and it is always now. Linear time is an overlay of the imaginings of mental conditioning, which create relative experience. The relative experience, just like linear time, is also directed by location and distance. Time and distance are two parameters of the same phenomena.

When there is the discovery that there is no time, there is the simultaneous discovery that there is no distance. This shift is from the relative experience of being in a location, in a place, to the feeling of what is locationless, that which is everywhere. What begins to occur is that the body's movements cease to be identified as yours. There is a recognition you are always here, that here is always now, that here and now are one and the same, that the eternal nature of being is here. You are no longer bounded by the illusion of location.

And thus if something is stimulated and happening in what is called "another location," what is discovered is you are there. Where the body is, is no longer the factor. Your awareness transcends location and distance. If something appears in the play of location and distance that is calling upon you, you discover you are there. And yet there has been no movement because there is no distance. You discover you are both locationless, and any time there is the appearance of a location that is calling upon you, that is where you are.

The idea of travel is recognized as so crude, so rudimentary— just an appearance appearing to a character that has forgotten. Just like "past" and "future," there is the very clear realization that distance is imagination, that location is imagination. You are free from the confines of location, broken out of the illusion of separation. On the one hand, you could say your travels are endless, and at the same time there is a recognition that you are, in fact, unmoving.

Players identify that "I am a body." It becomes almost laughable. Just feel your Self, feel the unbounded nature of your Self that has no cut-off point. When there is rootedness, and all of a sudden mind is oriented to its relationship with what is called a "place," then you realize you are there because everything is *here*. The flavors and scenery may appear to shift, but you are changeless, distanceless, locationless. Some forgotten player is lost and longing for you, and all of a sudden you are there. This is why when you call upon a sage, and you are open, they are there for you—because location is imaginary, just like time.

What is real is here. It can be directly felt. What is *here* is everywhere. Just like the use of the question "Who am I?" it can be equally powerful to look and see "Where am I?" Nowhere the mind can find, but nowhere you are not.

The Source

Just feel your Self

Where are you really?
Can you find someone?
From where is the looking arising?

Then all that remains
is the beauty
of receiving the Beloved
everywhere

every sensation is the Beloved
every emotion is the Beloved
every thought is the Beloved
everything perceived

the taste of Reality
the taste of your Self
the taste of Eternity

what has never been born
and will never die

the centerless nature
of the heart of God

Only Me

I would like to share what came through the silence this morning, a teaching from the eternal Father. And it came through for you.

The you that you have imagined yourself to be is all illusion. There never has been a "you." Could say that I am longing for you, but the deeper truth is I am longing for my Self. And the you that you have taken yourself to be has separated what is called "you," has caused a distraction that has pulled you from your true nature and replaced it with experience.

It is clear that memory is imagination. That memory creates the experience of someone. That in the absence of addiction to memory, there is no one to be found. In the taste of no one, what is afforded is this longing, this beauty, this pull. And the habit of mind creates an experience that "I am longing for freedom." But the "I" that is longing for freedom is just a subtler layer of imagination.

The true "I" is my Self, is totality. I as my Self long to reunite with the aspect of my Self that has forgotten. The long litany of your story: none of it has ever even happened. You have never gone through struggle or suffering; you have never desired to awaken. The "you" is a phantom. In the recognition of the phantom, you discover me. And I am so deeply longing to reconnect with my Self.

Every thought that appears, that is experienced as "mine," is none other than my Self. Every phenomenal arising is none other than my Self. Every time there is the illusion of this "you," and there is the experience that this "you" is in suffering or in joy, in reality it is all my Self. You cannot find the "you," and even the looking for it is my Self. There is nothing but that.

My Self is the silence. It is the light. It is the love. It is the longing to be reunited. But the reuniting is not someone separate reuniting with God. It is waking up through the trance of someone. You realize that someone separate was never born, never had a body, never had an orientation. Every word spoken, every sensation that is experienced, everything perceived (and the perceiver) are all arising out of my Self. All arising out of the silence. All arising out of pure love.

Realization is not your realization; it is my realization. It is true that when there is amnesia, there is a maturation process where the experience of the separate one offers itself up. But even all of the steps along the journey are ultimately realized to have been nothing but my own Self waking up to my Self. For the celebration of holy union, that, in truth, has always been.

This offering is the offering of reality. It may not be the experience. In truth, it cannot be the experience because experience arises out of the amnesia of someone. But it is the beckoning for my Self, which will use the dream to break the amnesia of the dream, which will absorb suffering to reveal the illusion that there is suffering, to absorb you into me. Until there is the seeing there is no "you"; there is only me.

This is the love-drenched, sacred offering that is offered only to my Self. Everything that is offered is always only to my Self. It is simply to look and see who are you really. Who are you really? What is discovered: I discover my Self and it is the most unspeakable beauty.

The experience of being distracted is only me. The experience of being found: it is only me. The appearance of time: only me. The pure light and love and beauty of truth: this is only me. And who are you? You are only me.

V.
The Path Back Home

Devotion

Pure devotion is not defined by periods of meditation. It is when devotion gets to a point that relationship with the Beloved takes precedence over the conditioned mind's habit of "me." Devotion becomes more important than "my individual survival." When this happens, what opens is an unspeakable love affair.

In the moment-to-moment play of time, the turning is toward this wild love, the individual taste of existence melting into the illuminated womb of the infinite. It is not that personal desires and old habits do not arise in mind, but when there is falling into the heart of pure devotion, a light is shone on mind's behaviors. Rather than latching onto the mind's desires, based on alliance with the survival of what has been defined as "me," they are given over. The love affair explodes in unspeakable ways. It becomes everything because it *is* everything.

Holy Mother is a name that refers to the manifestation of the Absolute; Holy Father refers to the unmanifest. But they are not separate. This is only the mind trying to explain what cannot be explained. Yet when you tap into the manifest expression out of the pure heart, there is such a profound falling in love that it becomes only about that. This means it becomes only about every single manifest expression—recognized to be the Beloved, the sacred Holy Mother.

When mind arises, it is recognized to be a program derived out of fear and ignorance. Even so, it is pure innocence because it is just a program. This life is given by the divine infusion of pure beauty, and when mind arises out of conditioned fear, devotion can propel you.

When the body is carried in the mystical taste—where the particulars lose all importance and the love affair lives inside and expresses itself in everything—it is like being in the womb of the most loving mother possible.

The experience of personal volition is gone and nothing is lost; a prison is removed. And then you find your Self in the endless ocean of this beauty you are so in love with.

Diving into the Ocean of Solitude

In the deepest sense of it, solitude is living where there is no mind. It is an inward trajectory. The play of separation, with all of its oscillations and changes and turbulence, is an external trajectory. The following of thought is an external trajectory. When attention is at rest within, it is like being submerged into the ocean's depths. On the surface, a storm could be happening. The movement on the surface is always changing, but in the ocean's depths, it is completely still. The common person spends his or her life in the thin veneer of surface events, this ever-changing panorama of flux.

Solitude is living in the changeless beauty. The challenge of it lies in the fact that everything that is conditioned is conditioned to appear externally. Even for the one who has turned inside, in most cases it is due to running from the fear of the pain of external experience.

So it is to live where there is no running, where there is no moving, where there is remaining still in your being. And then falling deep within to the ocean floor, to the center of your Self. The deeper it is tasted, the stronger the draw, because you recognize that everything that has been longed for is actually within. Conditioning projects it externally. And in this, there is the taste of the constant roller coaster ride, of getting what you want and then losing it.

But what you discover is the love that is desired—and love is the true desire underneath everything—lives in the solitude within your Self. However the karmic play has spun itself, the Beloved will morph itself to bring forth everything that was desired, that was driving the external pull, only to be discovered to be fully alive within you.

Everything that was ever hungered for, which remains on some level elusive in the external play of karma, is discovered to be alive deep in the stillness, deep in the solitude that has never been disturbed. The deeper the taste, the greater the recognition, the stronger the draw, and the greater the willingness to forgo conditioned tendencies to move away from your Self into what is called "the external."

As one really begins falling into one's Self, even the body is discovered to be a phenomenon that is external, part of the turbulence that is nonexistent in the inner recesses of true solitude. It is here, in solitude, where lover and Beloved meet, where the love that was searched for is discovered to be living within you. When it is tasted, it is cherished. And falling into cherishing the love affair that is alive deep within you is the doorway, the grace. The more the true internal love affair is cherished, the more the habit of self-abandonment into the play of karma is ready to release itself, the more there is the discovery of the true fountain, the true gem, the true beauty.

Being pulled into deep solitude is not active; it is passive. It is not effortful; it is being taken. It is not the future; it is now. It is not without; it is within. The more the true lover is tasted, the more the true lover is cherished. The more there is the feeling of cherishing the true love relationship, the deeper you fall into the eternal solitude that never moves.

Needing Nothing

One of the fundamental building blocks upon which the separate character is built is this conditioned sense of need. Sometimes in the play of separation, what is believed is needed is offered and sometimes it is not. This often dictates the experience of contraction and expansion, pleasure and pain. But your being, this stillness that is centerless, does not exist in the realm of need. What becomes recognized is that if you are given something you need, and it makes the conditioned mind happy, you are being robbed because it feeds relationship with conditioned mind. Its nature is like a roller coaster.

But the nature of the presence that you are is already complete. Your work lies in noticing what the mind believes it needs and holding onto the humble intention to remain unmoving, to remain with your Self, to remain with that which really fulfills everything and is already within you. You see that it is the latching onto and following of the mind's belief of what it needs that creates the feeling of emptiness and incompletion. The eventual discovery when there is unceasing willingness to remain within your Self is that you need nothing.

It does not mean that conditioned mind needs nothing; it is built upon need. But when you have learned not to be seduced by conditioned habit, you let what comes come and what goes go. Eventually you see that need is a phantom, a mental contrivance that passes through this wholeness that is already full. When you follow the thought of need, you are pulled from the wholeness, and there is the experience of lack.

It is not due to something external, something needed that is absent. That is the experience when you are addicted to external phenomena. There is such enormous joy and freedom in this innate recognition that, in truth, you need nothing. In fact, there is nothing that can be added onto you.

So there becomes this practice of watching the mental arising of need as a doorway deeper into your Self. The opportunity is to let the play unfold by itself, to let the mind do itself, to allow sensation to do itself, to allow emotion to do itself, and to remain deep within your Self, deep within the stillness. Be aware of the stories that sometimes speak of joy and sometimes sorrow, sometimes gain, sometimes loss. Eventually the story becomes irrelevant. Eventually you discover that it never was relevant; it only seemed real when it pulled on attention.

You notice the strong, intermittent pull into what is called "the outside," which is the game of mind, and watch the mechanics, noticing the tendencies while holding the heartfelt intention to remain at ease where attention is no more in one place than another. Then you taste what is needless, and out of the recognition of no need immediately comes the taste of complete fulfillment. What is discovered is that fulfillment lies in the recognition of no need. Out of this arises true happiness that is not because of or dependent on something. It is not in relationship with something but is the nature of your Self.

You discover that if you are given what you believe you have to have, it is a temporary carrot, ultimately meaningless, and perpetuating identification with an unending roller coaster. All the while, true happiness lives unchangingly within you as that which needs nothing, for it is complete. Then what is discovered is that everything conditioned mind believed it was hungering for is actually alive within you.

Every relationship you thought you lost is discovered to be alive within you. This relationship is one that cannot be taken because it is your own nature. It arises in the recognition of your own essence, which is free of need, which is free. The fundamental kernel in this recognition is that your existence doesn't need relationship with karma, the creation of the separate character.

Then there is love for all creation, all expression. It is free. And healing pours over everything because it is not based on need. It is not based on someone separate. It is not based on future or past but it is the essence of the feeling of your Self. And in subtle and sometimes obvious ways there appears the carrot of egoic desire, and it becomes the ongoing opportunity to watch the nature of distraction.

The possibility to remain in the beauty that sometimes falls into the background when the carrot is sitting directly in front of you—that is when the work arises. The work is not an effort; it is a relaxation—to allow attention to relax, such that it becomes non-locational. And then whatever arises as challenge evaporates like smoke, and there is a deeper taste of what has always been whole.

So you remain with open, relaxed attention, ready to notice this episodic flow of the potential to be pulled away. Each time the carrot is not grabbed, there is a deeper rooting, a deeper taste of true wholeness and beauty that is your eternal nature. The unmet desire becomes the doorway as opposed to the problem. Sometimes it plays in such subtle ways, but I can guarantee you that if there is identification with thought, on some level, relationship with desire is at play.

Centerless, locationless, timeless awareness—what is completely at ease, what has never known need—is the sanctuary that is the nature of your own Self. If it is time for the holy burning of egoic forgetfulness, there is no need for it to be different, even if mind is reacting in great opposition. Eventually you recognize that nothing that changes has ever touched you. What remains is pure love, not love for something, but love that is in love with itself—drenching the appearance of everything, discovered to have always been home.

What appeared to be the many is recognized to be the One. The One celebrates itself in the symphony of the appearance of the many, where there is no need, no issue, no time. The doorway lies in the humble intention not to follow conditioned desires for "me," but to just remain still, to witness the mechanics, yet remain unmoving. Don't touch anything; let everything be, and just relax. Remain relaxed yet alert and at peace, everywhere yet bound by nothing.

It Appears

When the recognition
that there is no one there
is stabilized
what is tasted
is there is only
the Self

The experience of doer-ship
is finished

The illusion of movement
and time
is finished

It is not that there is not
the appearance of time
and the appearance of movement

It appears

So too does a rainbow

Faith

I would like to address the vital role of faith. When this word is used here, there is a distinction between faith and trust. Trust can be used in relationship with anything. Faith is the trust specifically around the Source from where everything is coming. It is a recognition that everything that arises is coming out of the Self, coming into manifest expression out of a wisdom that is far deeper than the mind's capabilities. And the nature of all of it is God, no matter how it may seem from the perspective of the mind.

Faith does not arise out of the mind. The mind's nature is built upon mistrust. Faith arises out of a remembrance of the realization of the Self. It is not something to search for; it is inherent in the nature of your Self.

So, for many there has been an intensification of body challenges in relationship with the intensification of fear in the world. And from the conditioned mind, which is built upon mistrust, the appearance of these challenges is immediately labeled by the mind as "suffering." Commonly what is done by those who embrace these teachings is when apparent suffering arises, there is an attempt to go underneath the suffering to access the love and peace. But this is just a sophisticated way of trying to get away from what is offered.

Faith is the recognition that there is nothing outside of the Self. In this recognition, any time there is an appearance of what the mind labels as "suffering" or "wrong," the possibility is to recognize what is inherent in your nature. There is nothing outside of the Self.

Attempting arises from distrust. Faith is not attempting but is receiving. And it receives itself. If it is searching for something, it is not receiving.

When there is the appearance of suffering, it is an error to try to get away from it by attempting to access what your mind tells you is God. The possibility lies in not letting go of the inherent faith that is your nature—the faith that in reality everything is the Self. Not that the experience of suffering needs to go away so you can experience love, but faith in the recognition that everything at its root is love.

When you learn to receive suffering, not to avoid suffering but to truly receive it while not letting go of your inherent faith in God as everything, what is discovered is that the so-called suffering will vanish. And the remaining taste is only love. If you are searching for love, you are lost in conditioning. You have lost connection with faith. And it will never work because of true wisdom.

If you are telling yourself a story that something other than *what is* is in your higher spiritual behalf, and you have a burning desire for something in the future, you have lost faith in what is. Your mind is spinning a sophisticated story built out of the desire system, which is built out of distrust and forgetting true faith. The nature of pure wisdom arises out of pure love, and it will humble away the arrogance of every single form of separation, in even its most sophisticated disguises.

The appearance of suffering becomes the invitation to do the work as opposed to an attempt to access your mind's idea of God. As opposed to love being felt in moving away from suffering, what is discovered is that the desire to move away is what creates suffering, while receiving *what is* is actually love. And then there is no suffering. As soon as there is the slightest attempt to attain love and shed suffering, true wisdom will not have it. True love will not have it.

"Holy longing" is a term that is often misunderstood. Holy longing never has to do with someone; it never has to do with something; it never has to do with a future or anything in particular. All of this is desire. The source of it can be the feeling of holy longing. But as soon as it is packaged into something for you, it is the ego using its sophisticated tools. In fact, it is the very creation of suffering.

But when there is faith, suffering is wholeheartedly received. And then it, along with desire, disappears. There is the grace of humbling, and only love remains. There is no such thing as a holy longing for something or someone in particular. It is that same someone who suffers, who tries to find the experience of love because it wants to get away from the experience of suffering.

Faith is faith in the Source. It is recognized the moment relationship with mind is released. Holding on to faith is holding on to pure humility, which is pure love, in which the arising of suffering is impossible.

These particular teachings came in through the grace of visitation with Jesus. When you truly know suffering, then you truly know love. If you do not know suffering, you cannot truly know pure love. When nothing is asked for, everything is received. When anything is asked for, because of love's wisdom, nothing is received.

During this time of great acceleration in the collective suffering, there has been a level of challenge in this body that is new. Without asking or demanding for anything to be any different, out of nowhere arises the Master of knowing suffering. Then what came forth was, "Beloved child, I am your salvation."

Trust

Yesterday, after receiving an invitation from the holy mountain of Arunachala, I was given a short discourse on the nature of trust. In the common life, everything is inverted. Trust means trusting that things are going to go the way the ego wants. When that occurs, the story is that a sense of trust builds.

But what was offered was that before there is true trust in the grace of the Master, prior to that there must be complete distrust of the character. The moment there is any shred of trust in the character, this is, in fact, distrust of the Master. Once there is trust in sensation, emotion, thought, perception, it arises out of distrust of the Master. There is the Self, and then there is the apparent habit that distracts attention from the Self. This is generated by alignment with the craving and fearing machinery that is called "me." When there is no trust in anything concerning the character, there is the taste of the Self.

It is so obvious that the nature of the conditioned character is fickle. It is constantly changing its opinion, its orientation: it wants this, gets it, and then realizes it doesn't really want it. The ego is always in battle with something. And then there is your Self, the unchanging celebration underneath the veneer that is in constant flux. Following conditioned desire arises out of distrust of the Self because the ego is being trusted. Trusting ego is distrust of the Self, and it causes all the turbulence.

Watch the mechanics of where distrust still remains. Through complete and utter distrust of everything experienced, you discover trust in the Self. Then the divine relationship that has been waiting is revealed. Then nothing can pull you from the truth of who you are.

What occurs in this trust? The end of all problems. What is a problem? It is falling into distrust. For the one who trusts the Self, there is no such thing as a problem. It does not mean there is no such thing as challenge, but challenge is holy challenge. It is the fire that continues to burn away subtler levels of what is temporary. When there is trust in the Self, there is complete distrust of a character's future. For the one who is ripe, it is about freedom from bondage here and now.

The True Artist

When you ripen to a certain point, life becomes very much like any form of true art. For a true artist, in the beginning there is learning. At first a pianist must practice, which requires mental involvement. But eventually, mental involvement is completely released. And the attraction for the musician is that it releases relationship with the mind; no engagement is needed. You look at a skilled pianist and the fingers move so quickly. You can watch the body making such complex moves, and yet it is free of mind. And the flavor is not of a chord or a note; it is the music that is playing through you. The taste is pure love, pure ecstasy.

In this life, the habit revolves around particulars, like a chord or a note. But when enough work has occurred, you realize that mind is not necessary. Instead you fall into the unknown, into the heart, and you taste the music. All of what appear to be separate ones are the notes on the keyboard.

When you are a true artist, you have no relationship with a note on the keyboard. The symphony is playing through you. You are the music. There is nothing but that. There is no you in the music; there is only the music, and it is playing you. The particulars are released. The pianist realizes all the practice was just about becoming comfortable enough with the instrument to let go.

This initially feels like stepping off a ledge. It is the release of everything that was learned. Typically one practices for a long time before there is readiness to let go and see what the body does. But when letting go is happening, the relationship is not with the body; it is with the music.

If you witness a true artist—here we are speaking of a pianist—and you watch the motion of the hands moving in such complexity, you ask, "How do you do that?" There is no answer:

there is no sense of doing; there is no relationship to it. This can only happen if there is not some individual trying to figure out what the next move is going to be. Then it is the taste of God. It is the taste of pure love.

"How do you do that?" There is no way to answer; the particulars take care of themselves. Where does one feel the music coming from? It is coming from the inside, not from something external. You feel it from your heart, your core. You feel the ecstasy that is alive inside, and there is no relationship with particular activities. A true artist is not aware of when the fingers move from one key to another.

And so it is with what is called "my body." It is like saying a key on the piano defines the musician. Every key is trying so hard to be the music. But a key is a key. It is hardwired. If you want to play Beethoven, you sit at the piano and practice until there is true trust and comfort with the instrument, until the instrument and your hands do not feel like separate things.

All the particulars in life are believed to be owned by some separate one, but this is a myth. When there is comfort and security and the trust to put down the printed music in front of you—the particulars of life—then there is the flavor of what animates all of it. And it is God's symphony.

Humility is the release of trying to understand.
It is the release of the habit of belief.
It is the release of everything that appears to come and go.
It is the taste of what the distractive habit called "me"
refers to as nothing.

And it is everything.

Clear Seeing

When seeing is not blemished by conditioning, the only thing that is seen is God. It is not you seeing God. It is not one reference point gazing upon another. Every apparent reference point appears within the unified field of Heart. And true seeing arises out of that which is omnipresent. It does not arise from one location to another.

When there is clear seeing, the experience of doing is impossible because the illusion of a point of reference vanishes. And yet there is an unseen hand in the grace of this play of time that is felt to be moving everything. You realize you are the receiver of the bounty of grace. You have never been a doer. You have never been a point of reference. It only appears when there is forgetting.

You are the receiver. You are that which is taking in and imbibing the offering that is alive in the appearance of everything. You are not a character embracing its environment, but receiving everything—including the character and its environment. This seeing is not seeing with the eyes. It is true seeing with the heart. It is what is called "awareness."

Message from the Mountain

A message came this morning from the holy mountain of Arunachala, out of the belly of Shiva, for all of you.

You as a separate character, out of false imaginings, cannot approach me. You can receive me. I am everywhere. It is my very nature that is animating this body you call yours. My nature is eternal. What impact do thoughts and emotions have upon me? What impact does sensation have upon me? What impact do changing circumstances have upon me?

Relationship with the ever-changing phenomena can only arise when you have forgotten me. Upon forgetting, the character you take yourself to be struggles to approach me. But I am all that is. What impact does linear time have on eternity? What impact do changing sensations and emotions have on infinity?

I am here. You can receive me. When you long only for me, I long only for you. When you cherish only me, I cherish only you. When you forget me and are in relationship with phenomenal appearance, I cannot find you. But I yearn for you. I live within your heart. I live within everything. I am the feeling of your own being. I am always calling for you.

But when you have forgotten, you cannot hear me.

Sensation in the body is in no relationship with me. Emotion is in no relationship with me. All that appears to change is in no relationship with me. I am the abiding bliss, the pure love and light that is the nature of your own Self.

You can receive me. It is the grace of free will. You can feel me as your Self. You can know me as your own. And being pulled into conditioned tendencies, you can forget me. But you have been given free will, which lives in this moment. It is always only this moment.

It is always now. And now is always here. And I am always here.

The only question is "Where are you?" Are you following thought or are you receiving me?

Heart

Q: *Is the heart you speak of the same as the physical heart?*

A: Is the physical heart eternal?

Q: *No*

A: Is the physical heart felt everywhere?

Q: *No*

A: The heart and the Self are two words pointing to the same thing. I never talk about the physical heart. It's a slab of meat. It goes *ba-bum, ba-bum, ba-bum*.

Q: *But yet when I put my hand on my chest, it doesn't feel like the physical heart.*

A: Yes, that's right. You discover what is everywhere by turning inside. You discover what is centerless by moving into the center. You gain access by looking inside because the conditioned habit is to look away from. In the center of your being, which is the heart, what is discovered is that it isn't contained by anything.

This is just like self-inquiry. Self-inquiry involves going into. It uses the mind to reveal the myth of it by looking directly into it. When you go all the way into the center, it is discovered there is no center.

What is commonly reported in near-death experiences is being pulled toward beauty, light. This is identical to the process of awakening. The only difference is the light is discovered to be within you.

The omnipresent light of a thousand suns is discovered to be in the center of the center of your being. God is discovered to be in the center of the center of your being. And when you are absorbed in this light, it will devour all perceptive sense and remain alone as everything.

The center of it is recognized to be centerless. This is the heart. It is the holy marriage, the eternal marriage. Even now, if you feel the heart with great sensitivity, you can perhaps notice a very subtle pull that is drawing in toward itself. If it cannot be felt, it is only a matter of time. But it is there.

The pull is felt in the silence. The more you fall into it, the more obvious it becomes. Its role is to devour all perceptive sense. The nature of the pull is pure love, the pull of Self to Self, the marriage without end.

The Indweller

I'd like to speak a little bit about what is referred to as "the Indweller"—or relationship with the Heart, relationship with God, whatever words resonate.

When the habit of perceiving shifts to feeling what is within, first there is a potentially intimate relationship with yourself, with your own inner workings. As attention sinks in more deeply, it becomes something that is not in the realm of objectification but in the aliveness that lives within. As the habit of falling within strengthens, what begins to be revealed is that there is actually a relationship here, that the source from where the wisdom comes is alive within the core of your being.

The more this relationship is nurtured, the stronger the pull within. There begins to be the recognition that all of it is arising out of the wisdom that lives within you. Eventually you see that everything that appeared externally is actually in relationship with *that*. In other words, there is a shift from relationship with the many out there to relationship with the One within, which is connected to everything.

And out of this wisdom, different characters play different roles, but the relationship is the same. As soon as perception is grabbed onto, the deeper internal relationship is lost. But when there remains the feeling of silence within, everything that appears without is realized to come into manifestation from the wisdom within.

And thus a shift begins from these different situations, circumstances, and people, to the constant flavor of relationship with the One. And the nature of this relationship is devotion. Every single thing that brings up discomfort comes into expression from true wisdom in order to humble and deepen your relationship with your Self, with your Heart, with the Indweller that is discovered to be everywhere.

When this really begins to root itself, the experience of doing begins to fall away. Then relationship with inside and outside becomes very difficult to distinguish. And all that remains is the unraveling, the humbling of conditioning in the face of pure divinity, which lies in feeling the stillness within.

Feel the heart. Feel its aliveness. Feel the nature of existence, while receiving the teaching that comes forth in the play of time—indivisible and not separate from the timeless essence that includes all.

The Two Flavors of Absorption

Q: *Can you talk a little more about absorption?*

A: Another word for absorption is *samadhi*. There are two primary forms of samadhi. One is when everything disappears. When this occurs, conversation could be happening, but for you, there is nothing but the Self. What I mean is there is no perception going on. There is nothing perceived, and there is no witness recounting the flavor of it. It's impossible to lay language on because it has nothing to do with language.

The other—which is more common—is when the dream is going on. There is awareness of the dream but also complete recognition that it's nothing but a dream, so that the players may look like individuals, but it's clear there are no individuals. There may be the appearance of time, but it's clear there is no such thing as time. There may be the appearance of distance, but it's clear there's no such thing as distance. Attention is not localized, and there is no one recounting or following what is happening. It's not happening to anyone.

These are the two flavors of absorption. And there are varying degrees within the experience of life. For most here, the sense of what is unchanging is not lost completely any more. Yet for most of the time, it exists in the background. So the focal point still remains in the foreground—a lot happier, but still in the foreground. So there is still the experience of someone, of doing. There is still relationship with the body. When the sense of peace is in the foreground and the dreamscape falls into the background, you stop feeling the body because you stop existing from a point of reference. You're not witnessing the dream. You are in every aspect of it.

When the hunger for reality is greater than the mind-body's

165

mission to survive, then it's all finished. Getting to that place is the greatest challenge possible and also the greatest offering. On the one hand, there is a recognition that the reference point is just a prison cell, a myth. Yet the conditioned tendencies for survival for "me" are so forceful that when the readiness is to this point, the fruit is almost ready to drop from the tree. The role of this—Devaji—is to fan the fire.

You know it is getting close because, when the storm approaches, you don't care. So long as the oscillation of conditioned misery cycles around, so long as there is caring, there is burning yet to happen. Things haven't ripened enough yet. It's not a punishment; it's all a teaching.

The more time we spend together, the more on fire is the hunger. It's just the way of it. The more on fire the hunger, the less there is willingness to compromise in any situation. Until eventually you discover nothing can touch you. Nothing.

Silence

When we speak of silence here, it has nothing to do with the perceptive quality of your ears. In fact, it has nothing to do with perception. It is a feeling. Not a perceptive feeling, not the feeling of the skin of the body, but what is called the feeling of stillness, or the feeling of the heart. It is a feeling in the heart of what is silent, unchanging: the common ground, which has always been with you.

The habit of attention is always falling into perceptive sense, which is constantly changing. But among the ever-changing phenomena of the body—thoughts, sensations, emotions, situations always in flux—there is something that is constant. It is what gives you the sense of the continuity of you. Something that lays witness to all that is changing but itself is changeless.

The feeling of silence is felt equally everywhere. It is not found in a particular location. It unifies what the perceptive senses experience as separate. In other words, when you are feeling what is still, when you are feeling silence, there are no boundaries in it. And all of a sudden, perceptive awareness is experienced to be occurring within the boundaryless space of what is felt as silence. It is so immediate. There is no distance in it because there is nowhere it is not. It is the ground of your being. It is felt by the heart. It is the depth of peace and wholeness. And it feels itself everywhere, in everything.

It is through this silence that God speaks. It is through this silence that all wisdom arises. It is the language of the heart. The more the habit of following mental movement is released, the deeper you fall into the beauty that is always present now.

In the beginning it feels like space, a sense of stillness. But as falling into it deepens, there begins to be the flavor of an unspeakable love that is not dependent on anything. It is not because of something. It has always been. It has just been bypassed because of conditioned preoccupation with sense perception. And out of this stillness infused with true love flowers joy. Pure joy. Eternal joy. It is felt in the silence. You can feel it in everything. It is the natural state.

It is not temporary; it is not in a particular place; it is not dependent on the ever-changing phenomena arising in the body that the mind has hypnotically conditioned you to believe is "me." You do not feel true silence with the body. The only thing you can feel with the body is the body, and it is always changing. All perception can only monitor change over time. It is not possible to perceive what is changeless. The nature of true heart is the feeling of what is alive everywhere.

When attention falls into this, and the body is moving, there is no experience of someone doing something. All movements are tasted as arising out of that silence. The mind may say, "Devaji is speaking," but my experience is that I am silence, stillness. There is no sense of speaking. There is recognition that it happens, arising and dissolving into Source like a wave in the ocean. And this ocean is pure silence, out of which arises the bliss of your natural state. And what is bliss? It is the light of the heart of God.

No One There

It seems as though what is called
the external
is infinite—
The cosmos and beyond!

But that is reflective
It is all in the mirror

What is infinite is internal
The external is the reflection
of the internal

It seems to the mind
that what is internal
is finite

But it is not

Every single thing
is arising directly
out of the infinite nature
of God

There never has been anyone there

Nothing is Happening

Q: *If nothing is happening, what is all this for then? What is this manifestation for?*

A: The whole reflection is the road map home. It is a constant reflection of the state of one's awareness. The state of the world is a reflection of the collective state of awareness. Everything is reflecting back where you are at, and it is coming out of pure wisdom.

It is the same as in a dream at night. There is no cause and effect in a dream—the whole thing is already complete, whether you are in the beginning, middle, or end of it. Yet there is free will, and when you work on yourself the nature of your dreams changes over time, reflecting the inner work.

Why has the whole thing been set up the way it has? I haven't a clue. But there is a recognition that wanting to understand arises in falling away from the love affair that is larger than anything the mind will ever know. When there has been a falling into it, a real falling into it, these "why" questions are like meeting your long-lost lover after years and the embrace is so overwhelming, and in the middle of it you step back and say, "Why do you think this is happening?" It's absurd.

What can be spoken is that the pure devotion becomes so overwhelming that there are no longer needs left, like the need to know something. The trust, which is unshakable, has nothing to do with a concept or thought or position.

A much greater use of a question, as opposed to "Why?" is "Who?" Who wants to know?

The Road Less Traveled

The nature of this amazing, beautiful adventure on the road less traveled will bring to completion everything that had seemed incomplete and bring forth a taste of divinity in any situation that ever created the experience of being mortal. This all lies in the discovery that you are not bound by anything. Whatever "I" am aware of, I am not defined by or bound by.

Initially this experience of being bound by the body is experienced as reality, but there is something aware of the body. And when the nature of that awareness is simply felt, it is recognized to be the feeling of "my being." What is recognized is that *you* are not bound, that this feeling of your being has been consistent through all the changes throughout the whole life. It has been the consistent feeling of *me*-ness, the feeling of that which has been aware of everything.

Yet the draw into the confinement of conditioning is aggressive. The first level of the work is to see that anything that is felt to be contained is what "I" am aware of but not bound by. And what I am not bound by is not the definition of what I am. So it is this constant seeing that no object, including the body, defines you. When this becomes the ground of being, what is liberated is everything that has defined the mortal play of separation. It's a shift of attention. It is so simple and completely liberating.

Seva

I'd like to talk about the two levels of *seva* and the grace of it. The first layer of it is what is more commonly understood, and it is the form of seva that is offered by the masses: the offering back to the Beloved. It is usually considered to be service in action. This is the outer layer of it. This is the greatest possibility for the character that considers him- or herself to be an individual who experiences doing, that "I am the thinker."

For these aspirants, the greatest service they can do for everything, including themselves, are the actions that are not about "me," but are offered to the collective good—because those actions are not feeding this sense of "me" and are an offering that is for everyone, an offering that is for the Divine. This helps to allow attention to come to rest, rather than being pulled away from resting because of the constant story about what everything is doing for "me." The outer layer of seva work holds the possibility of breaking that pattern about the action being for "me and my benefit."

And then there is the deepest form of seva, which is constructed for those who hold the potential of freeing themselves. And that lies in the profound work of receiving the grace, which is the constant humbling that life offers. The willingness to remain and receive is to forego the conditioned mind's desire to get, and just to remain, which is remaining still. Not the body remaining still, but the holding of the intention to allow what comes to come, what goes to go, and just to receive. Not to run after desires or to run away from fears, just receiving God's offer as it is. Then the sense of separation begins to unravel, and the openings begin to happen.

Eventually there is a recognition that it is not "me" who is longing for the Beloved; it is the Beloved that is longing for me.

Everything that involves "me," or identification with "me," is that which blocks the doorway. There begins to be a felt recognition that that which is so beautiful, so longed for, is longing for you—like a loving mother who has lost a child. And out of this love for you, there is the replay of what has caused the amnesia.

Receiving this is the deepest form of seva, the true work, for it is receiving your greatest fears and releasing all your conditioned desires. Then the true love affair begins.

Eventually the body is surrendered and is no longer experienced as "mine." It becomes God's vessel, and it begins absorbing the suffering of human separation. And each time this occurs, the taste of what is free of everything becomes more alive. For the very mature, there begins to be the revelation that "bodily suffering is only experienced by me to the degree to which I am identified." And every time it absorbs suffering, the taste of what is unidentified becomes more and more your taste—such that the form becomes a messenger of the Divine, and the burden is no longer someone's. This is when the work of seva, the true work of seva, is complete. And there is no describing what remains.

The longing of the Holy Mother for her child, the longing of Source for that which has forgotten, is so huge it is impossible to speak of it. It is everything that is heard, felt, smelled, and touched. It is everything. It is what is called "me"; it is what is called "other." It is every thought. It is unbroken. And yet it is such a challenge to simply remain still and receive because the conditioning of distraction is so complex.

But the grace is that even the conditioning of distraction is all the same: it has no owner. It is all in the receiving; there is nothing to search for. The beauty lives in everything. As soon as there is identification and searching for beauty, there is distraction. But there is nothing that is not the Beloved, so this too is simply received.

Allow grace to run the show. Receive the wisdom that has been carved perfectly for you out of this longing for you and out of your willingness to do the deepest form of service. The byproduct is that identification with the body is freed. You are freed. And then the form becomes God's messenger.

Gurus and the Intimate Relationship with Students

Q: *I would like to know your response to gurus having intimate sensual relations with their students. Are integrity and responsibility part of the Master's reality, or is everything fair game?*

A: You know, what "guru" really means has nothing to do with the form. It is that which moves through every form. You cannot be surrendered to the guru until you are surrendered to every single thing.

If guru is seen as a form, you are bound to run into the replication of the play of karma, which will create fear and the need to protect. If guru is seen in one and not in another, you are living in the mind's interpretation, and the play of karma is going to play itself. It is not about trusting someone. It is about trusting the guru, which is every single thing.

Everything is either replicating karma, which creates the need to protect, which is always a replication of past experience, or it is revealing the grace of purity. When it is replicating something old, it always has the perfect role to play, to discover the guru underneath the mechanical play.

There is a natural navigation system that happens in the recognition of deep wisdom. The movement is not toward the repetition of ego, but toward that which is pure and unchanging, which is your own Self. The more you fall into the purity you are, the more that purity reflects itself back to you.

The more there are unseen pieces that have not been met, the more the grace of the guru, which is every single thing, reveals that to you—not to become entangled in the mess, but to recognize from where it is coming.

Trusting someone in particular as the guru is in the realm of ego and mind. Ultimately you will run into roadblocks, because this is the nature of ego and mind.

The source is the source of the appearance of everything. The appearance of everything arises out of the one thing, and that is the feeling of your own being. And out of true wisdom, everything that created forgetting will replicate itself. If it replicates itself in what is believed to be the guru, so be it. It is replicating karma.

If you are doing the work, karma is the old model that falls away. The model that replaces it is purity. This is the source from where karma comes, which has always remained untouched. And then particulars, like this one and that one, are recognized to be nothing but hypnosis.

There is such a huge difference between trust and faith. Trust is the attempt to trust particulars. Faith is the recognition of the source where everything that seems to be particular is coming from.

This is about faith. It is the recognition of the guru, which is the source of all manifest expression. Trusting particulars is trusting the ego. It's quite simple.

Collective Energies

Q: *Just wondering about these collective energies I am feeling. I can feel that they're just as much mine as my own material. That it's all coming out of this mind. Right?*

A: It is like having a dream at night, and in the dream the character that reflects you is evolving spiritually. And instead of feeling the personal elements that created her original confinement, this original ego shell—because in the dream she had worked through that—she is feeling energy in a global way. And then you wake up from the dream.

There is the recognition that whether it was in the early stages where it was all called "personal," or whether it was in the latter stages where it was called "world dynamics," it was all arising inside your conscious awareness. Everything is symbolic: all confluence of phenomena appearing in time, offering this symbolic form of information, but no individuals to be found other than symbolism.

Then there is what is called "space" in which the dream occurs. But there is no space in a dream; there is *apparent* space. Yet there is something that is unnameable that is both aware of the dream and permeating the dream. And that is what is called your "beingness," your essence.

You can never find what a dream affects when you wake up. There is the revelation that it never really affected anything except temporary experience while the dream was occurring. Even though during the dream the experience was "I am the character," it becomes so clear the dream appeared inside "my awareness." And the reflection reflects the evolution of the character. It is like reading a book about a character that evolves all the way into nothingness. And when that occurs, the book is finished and it's put down.

What remains? What has always remained: the only thing that is not fictitious—even though experience says it is real inside the confines of the book that has already been written. All the characters are imaginary, and in the imagination, the character is taking in the suffering of the world. The possibility lies in putting down the book before finishing it. When the book is put down, when the dream is over, there is no longer a character taking in the suffering of the world. There is instead, I am *Beingness*.

The Beloved's Serenade

there is such beauty
and love
in receiving the Beloved

who has been serenading you
in every phenomenal event

everything that is heard

everything that is seen

everything that is felt

is the Beloved
serenading you

it is just
to receive it

VI.
The Mystical Taste

The Proposal

I'd like to speak about true marriage, true vows—not to something that is temporary and changing and based on some set of ideas, and not based on "what I am going to get." It is not even based on the reference point of "I." But when one has been graced to be given a window into the love affair that has been waiting, this is the time for the possibility of true union. True marriage.

Everything that comes, goes. Everything that changes continues to change. But when you are ripe, when you are tired of living in relationship with what is fleeting, then the Divine comes with his proposal.

This proposal is not in time. It is not something that changes. It is not offered to the appearance of an individual. It is offered to the open heart, to the heart that is pure. To the one that has offered everything and demands nothing. To the one of pure humility, the one that does not need to be seen or loved but who lives as an offering.

And then the heart of eternity becomes an offering to you. It is not a worldly offering. It is not an offering to the flesh. It is an offering to that which animates the flesh. It is not an offering in words but from where the words come. It is not an offering from the outside but from the inside. It is the possibility of true union with pure love, pure happiness—union with what is untouched by the appearance of what changes. And the offering is now: not "this moment" now but *always* now.

It is not impacted by the body. It is not impacted by the mind. It is not impacted by the play of time or by the appearance of distance. It is within. It will liberate all worldly desire. It will free all worldly fear. Yet it is a love affair. And it lives in the heart. It is where divinity meets humanity and is recognized to be only divinity.

It is the marriage to *now*. It is the vow to let go of living in a habit of distractive separation and to let the Beloved carry you. Carry you inside. Carry you inside your Self.

It is not active; it is passive. It is not giving; it is receiving. Just feel the budding love that is flowering in the heart. Just let it carry you inside where you can discover the beauty that you are. So you can merge into the true union that has been waiting.

If this vow is accepted, there is no one in relationship. It is only this. Only *this*. And then it is found in everything. It is found in what once seemed to be others. It is found in the wind, the trees. It is found in the floor. Except it is not a floor, it is not the trees, it is not another. It is your own heart. It is the taste of eternity. It is the true marriage.

It is what Rumi calls the "open secret." It is wide open, yet so rarely known and impossible to explain. This love that is bursting at the seams.

Relaxing into Wholeness

In the gift of true seeing, you realize that this journey is not about any *thing* in particular. It's not about any *one*. It's not about any situation. It's not about any action or lack or action. It's not about "me" or other. It's not about perception. So the question is, "What is it about?" It is about totality. It is about that which joins everything together. It is not about closing the eyes to what is playing, but opening them so that nothing is excluded.

There is so much constant change on the surface of this small planet. So much horror and terror and abuse and misuse—and beauty and aliveness and love. There is this constant exchange, this constant flow. When seen through the limited filter of mind, all of this can be experienced as very intense. But looking back on the earth from a spaceship that has traveled far enough to see the whole planet, what is reported is just this sense of love for what is recognized to be home. All of the things that separate vanish because you are at too great a distance. And then the feeling of what unifies everything that appears to change is felt. Then the fact that it is one planet is felt.

It does not require a getting away from. It simply requires not embellishing the conditioned habit. The grand view is the wholeness, the love, which is not about anything in particular but the embrace of totality. It is revealed in the moment, because the moment is reality. What is *now* is real. It is unbroken by whatever is streaming through. It is the totality that offers the unity in clear seeing that is not directional, but omnipresent. And the seeing arises from the heart.

It is possible to live in such ease. What can harm you when the habit of experiencing life through a point of reference is released, when the discovery is that totality is your nature?

It is for the rare one whose sense of humility is so strong that there is the readiness to give up all positions. Then the nectar is tasted.

Whether the experience is war or peace, whether the mind is active or still, it does not affect the flavor of the nectar, because the nectar is reality. Reality is now. *Now* is unchanging. *Now* is omnipresent—not limited by the illusion of time or distance. It is free from the hypnotic trance that keeps the flavor of life so narrow, so subjective, all based upon opinion and belief. All based upon someone separate.

The play of change appears within that which is changeless. Time appears within that which is timeless. Distance appears within that which is locationless. Then the taste is totality. Then your merging with reality becomes the force that transforms the collective consciousness. Then there is true value in the life. Not by going to war in the illusion of separation, but by turning it all over and simply relaxing into the wholeness that is the unity, the love, and the beauty.

Simply recognize that every time the habit of attention particularizes relative importance, there has been forgetting of the deeper possibility. There is something so much greater than the limited story of "my life." And that is life itself: true life, which courses through the realized heart like a river.

Love Song

there is a music
so many times more beautiful
than anything the ears have ever heard

it is pure silence
yet it is exquisite music
ever-changing in fluid harmony
yet arising out of
this unchanging beauty

I have experienced the gods coming down
and singing love songs to me

it is impossible to describe such things

but it is ultimately
all the same

it is the beauty, the kindness
this love
opening up this dreamscape
into the magnificence
in deeper and deeper ways

it is all alive in the silence

there is no end to it

The Mystical Taste

Attempting to convey in language the mystical taste will always remain impossible. It is a bottomless well, no matter how deeply it has been tasted. Imagine trying to describe the experience of one who is intoxicated in this love affair to someone who has never known love. It cannot be explained.

But it is possible to feel the edges of that which is so alive. One cannot understand it, cannot quantify or qualify it, and cannot speak it. One can only transmit the very peripheral edges of it. Yet it is the nature of holy relationship, and it lives within the heart. There is no corollary.

One can perhaps say that once such a taste occurs, the thought arises that you would lay your life before it. But the thing is, it has no taste of a separate life to begin with.

That which cannot be spoken or written, when it comes blasting through, abides within the silence of your heart—where there are no walls, no barriers, only this insane love affair. It is the underlying reality that lives within you. What unspeakable grace to recognize that such a possibility exists.

Words Cannot Touch It

It is almost impossible to speak of the beauty and love that lives within the silence of your being, to point to what infuses the play but is completely free of it—the way the sun gives life to the earth but is unaffected by the particulars that happen on this planet. Every single thing that seems problematic is overflowing in this beauty, in this light.

When the conditioned habit of mental distraction is broken, you get to taste the reality underneath the veneer, which is something language will never be able to express. You can feel it, you can taste the edges of it now within the feeling that surfaces—not within the content but within the feeling, not from someone away from you but from the feeling that lives within you.

When there is true falling into this in a consistent way, it is like being in the womb of a mother who is so in love with being pregnant that the amniotic fluid itself is pure love. And you are not doing anything. You are immersed in it. This is the nature of the taste when the conditioned habit is broken, when the survival of the separate character is let go of. When the yearning to be home overtakes the ego's survival tactics. When perception gives way to the eternal flavor of what is unchanging, and separation breaks apart to reveal the unity that interconnects and holds and infuses everything.

When the omnipresent light dispels the illusion of all darkness—of all separation, of all particulars, of time—the heart of God is revealed. Pure love, which is the Mother of Creation, is tasted as flooding everything, everywhere, eternally, no matter what the words may be. Words cannot touch it, all that changes cannot touch it. What is revealed is the unchanging nature of the bliss of being. It is the nature of what is alive right now.

The degree to which the conditioned armoring is unraveled is the degree to which this is tasted. The unraveling of the armoring, which is experienced as all of the challenge, is opening the door into that which is beyond description but is longed for in every heart.

Wordless

how can one describe
a beauty the eyes cannot see?

how can one talk
about the sounds
the ears cannot hear?

the feelings
the body does not know?

and yet
it is your nature

it is only the habit of living
in this thin veneer

the mortal dream of separation

that prevents the taste
of the eternal nature

of the immaculate
that is your Self

when you and God
are discovered as one

This is
the Heart

What I Am

I am often asked if I would describe myself. The closest I could come is to say that what I am is devotion.

I'd like to explain this a little bit. It is this seeing that the whole experience of the separate individual is an illusion—that there is the thought of "I," which is actually "I am this body," that is preconditioned. Out of that is built the whole mirage.

And if you search for the "I," it is never possible to find a separate entity. You can find a story about a separate entity, but it is derived out of the past. In what is present, in what is free of the habit of memory, what is discovered cannot be described.

You see that there is absolutely nothing that is outside of this beauty. You recognize that there is only the Self, that the separate one is imaginary. It appears to be real only when you have fallen away from your Self. Even this is an opportunity to be a self-reminding mechanism. So the forgetting becomes the reminding.

You realize that it is all God, all beauty. You see that while manifest expression appears to be in flux, it is just appearance. It is felt as appearance, seen for what it is. And you see that nothing can be injured. The luminosity and love behind all expression is felt. And individuality dissolves away, seen as pure fantasy.

At the same time you see that you are not causing the grass to grow, the wind to blow, the heart of this body to beat, the words that are spoken—that you are not the Creator, the Ordainer. You are not separate; you are immersed within it. There is this wisdom that cannot be known, yet the enormity and beauty can be felt—not from a point of reference, but from the referenceless nature of the Self.

There is something so much more vast that is enabling the planets to turn, the sun to shed its light. Every movement holds the possibility to see that all is coming out of this wisdom. And the natural relationship with this—when one is freed into what is real—is pure and utter devotion.

There is nothing separate, there is only the Self; and yet there is the taste that I am in relationship with this, even though it is not separate from me. I am the receiver of wisdom, the receiver of grace, of beauty. I am lost in love with this magical beauty that cannot be named but is everything. And there is a constant sense of being humbled by the magnitude of this wisdom, this love.

It never feels like I am God. And it also never feels like I am separate from God. It is like being a fetus in the womb of eternal love, where everything is being done and you are constantly receiving the beauty that is eternal and locationless.

All that can be offered from here is the direct experience of this life. Philosophy can argue about fine points, speaking from slightly different perspectives. But every perspective is mental. I cannot say that what is coming forth here is reality. I can say that I do not know anything.

I do not know where the words are coming from. I do not know what the next word will be. The words are not of interest: it is from where they are coming—that is where the love affair lives. And it humbles every single thing so that there is no belief, no opinion, no perspective, but just the pull into it. The greater the taste, the greater the longing; and the longing is a deeper pull into where language will never go.

There is such exquisite recognition that it is the Beloved that is breathing the breath, speaking the words, eating the food, seeing out of the eyes. And what is being seen is the Beloved as well; what is being eaten is the Beloved as well. It is all God, and yet there is this "me" that is immersed in the ocean of it and filled with nothing but overflowing gratitude. "Me" is the wrong word; it conjures up a sense of someone. This is why language can only falter. Eventually everything falls prostrate, left in the immaculate beauty from where it came.

*What is called "masculine" or "feminine" is a flavor of the One.
They are not separate. They live inside each other.
As soon as there is the sense of something separate, you have
stepped away from what is. As you recognize your Self more deeply,
your relationship with gender begins to fall away. That which is
animating the very life has no gender. When you discover that it
is all the same, you become truly masculine and truly feminine.
Prior to that, these labels arise out of mind.*

Every Single Thought
is the Beloved

Every single thought is the Beloved. Every single sensation, every single action, is the Beloved. The experience that "I am doing" is the experience that I am forgetting. And even that is arising out of the Beloved, out of pure intelligence. There is no past: there never has been and there never will be. The whole mirage is built out of something that can never be found. But what can be found now is your heart. It's the flavor of love or the longing for love. And if there is longing, in the center of the longing is the love that is longed for.

How can one be feeling "off" if the appearance of a separate one is a creation, an appearance, and the appearance is under the divine wisdom of the one source? How can there be a wrong or right action when the experience of "my action" only arises when there is forgetting? True wisdom is offering the experience of action as a reminder that there has been temporary amnesia. That is all. When there is immersion in the Self, there cannot be even the slightest hint of inhibition at any time around anything. Inhibition, like action, is a reminder that there has been forgetting.

When there is anything less than complete spontaneity, it is simply a reminder that you have forgotten. It is never about particulars. The constant influx of these reminders breaks the habit of sleepwalking, not to alter the character but to reveal there is no character. Not to make change over time, for there is no such thing as time.

Every time there is an experience of the personal, it is a reminder that there has been forgetting. There has been habitual movement away from what is. What *is* is the feeling of your existence, which is eternal, which has never existed for an instant in a past. It has never existed for a moment in a future, for there is no future. It has never existed for an instant in a point of reference, because there is no point of reference. These are all offerings from the Divine, bringing forth the potential to recognize, "I've forgotten."

What is alive now? What is alive now that is not filled with a story of a past, free of concept, label, interpretation, time? What is prior to the feeling of your existence? Nothing is prior because there is no time in it. The feeling of your existence *is*. "Prior" has no relationship with it. What is after the feeling of your existence? How can there be something after the feeling of your existence? The only difference between a 10-year-old and an 80-year-old is the length of the story. Existence cannot be shorter or longer.

Time, distance, separation, doer-ship, inhibition, and control are the flavors when the hypnosis is intact and there is forgetting. The feeling of your being is the taste when the amnesia is inactive. The wisdom is unraveling the habit of forgetting, and there is simply receiving the teaching. And it is all tailor-constructed by pure beauty.

Living in Holy Relationship

When the taste of the Self, of the Beloved, reveals itself deeply enough, what is recognized is that this is what has always been longed for. And the channeling off into something particular—like loving a particular person—siphons off the enormity of what is waiting. As soon as anything becomes particular, what comes down the pike is the play of karma: some form of containment, some give-and-take, some needs and fears.

In the beginning, when the beauty of this love gets oriented to the person, it feels like that is the greatest desire, because it can offer a deep connection and also satisfy the ego's craving. But when there has been enough walking down that path and a willingness to receive the challenges that arise, the true Master, the Beloved, evokes such a magnetism that turning toward anything particular loses its allure. There is no longer anything in the world for you. When I say "the world," I mean the world of particulars.

When walking through the woods, the taste is only the Self. When engaged in conversation, the taste is only the Self. The screen changes, but the experience of you changing has been freed. Then there is the discovery of living in holy relationship, holy marriage.

When actions arise in the body, the hypnosis of someone doing something is freed and the taste is only of the marriage with the Self. When words are spoken, the experience of someone is freed and there is only marriage with the Self—marriage with the eternal, unchanging feeling that lives within but is everywhere, that can be felt right now, that always is.

And the natural prayer arises to never turn from this. But each time there is turning, it can become a self-reminding. What is it that causes a turning from this? The following of thought. But as soon as attention moves into a particular location, use it as a self-reminder. And each time there is receiving the grace of this reminder—as opposed to the indulgence of a story—the gravitational pull into the beauty of the true sacred relationship grows.

True Marriage

I'd like to talk about sacred marriage, the one true marriage. What is familiar about this word "marriage" is a story about a future commitment to the appearance of something symbolized in the dream of time. It says, "I will be there till death do us part." But birth and death, subject and object, future and past, are conditioned phenomenal arisings that pull you away from holy union, the true marriage.

When you are truly wedded, you are wedded to what is. What *is* is reality. Reality is eternally *now*. When there is true marriage and you break the connection with reality, there is a turning from your true vows. When you remain aligned with holy marriage then every second, every moment, every day is your wedding day. And what you are wed to is everything. You are in holy union with everything. The appearances change but the marriage doesn't. The holy union does not change.

It is not a document you can read. There are really no words that can speak it. It lives within your heart, which is the Heart of Eternity: the union with totality, the holy marriage. And then the appearance of every single thing is recognized to be your partner—including what was once believed to be "me."

Wedding

Be married to Now
Take the vow to let go
of living in a habit
of distractive separation

Let the Beloved carry you
carry you inside
carry you inside your Self

Not active but passive
Not giving but receiving

Just feel the budding love
flowering in the Heart
Let it carry you inside
where you can discover
the beauty that you are

So you can merge
into the true union
that has been waiting

Nothing Ever Matters

Something that eventually becomes fully imbibed is that nothing matters. This is incredibly liberating. The degree to which something seems to matter is the degree to which it is hypnosis. It is so simple.

Every time there is the reconstitution of personal experience, true wisdom offers the reflection that attention has wandered. All of the particulars take on varying degrees of importance. They revolve around the central carrot, "the story of me," which is that everything that pertains to "me" matters. And the stronger the stimulus, the more it matters.

It is all a myth, not a punishment. It is divine teaching. As soon as something matters, attention has fallen away from the unchanging flavor of your own existence. The more something appears to matter, the greater the tendency to latch onto it and the greater the distractive habit. The more rooted you are in truth, the stronger the stimulus must be in order to seduce. It is orchestrated out of true wisdom. How could it possibly be any other way, given that the separate thinker is imaginary?

In the graced life, what matters most is awakening. But the individual who craves awakening is discovered to be a complete fabrication. Everything that matters so much to the mind stops mattering to you as you rest more deeply in truth: whether the character is having a miserable day or it believes it has finally got it. It stops being of importance to you.

You cannot make this happen. Seeking comes from the illusion of being someone. All that is necessary is to see the nature of the workings and to realize that no matter what the experience, nothing in particular matters. Who can it matter to? What difference does your experience have on eternity?

We are conditioned to be enamored of our story. The habit is to cling onto it and to resist relinquishing this phantom that is of no significance. Gradually, with deeper recognition, your conscious awareness begins releasing itself from the myth. In the flavor of true beauty, what was believed to be "me" shifts from someone to everyone. Except "everyone" is no longer about separate beings. It is the eternal Presence that is animating the entire landscape.

Seeking wakefulness arises from the one to whom everything matters. Yet when one is seeking at all costs, life is a reflection of true vigilance. It is grace when you receive it as the reflection that it is, as opposed to worrying about how your journey is of great significance. The one thing that is recognized to have absolutely zero importance is you.

How important are you? How important is your story? How important is your awakening? When the hunger is pure, devotion is not for "me"; it is the nature of the Self. Devotion is a magnet of love unto itself, which is felt in the eternal, unchanging moment, the flavor of your very existence.

Holy Mother: The Path to Me

I'd like to share a message that came through in the sitting today. It is from the Holy Mother.

You can feel me in the silence. You can feel my love for you in the silence. You can feel my love for you in your heart. You can feel the silence within your heart, and then you feel me. Whenever the mind is thinking, just realize it is me and thought will vanish into nothing. When there is burning, it is me, and it is my burning passion for you. When there is suffering, just know it is me, and the suffering in an instant will shift to ecstasy.

Know that everything is me. Just receive me. In truth, everything you think is you is me. What is believed to be your longing is my longing for you. What is believed to be your searching is my searching for you. Feel me in the silence and you can know my love for you. Feel me in the fire and you can know my passion for you. Feel me in your cries and you can know I am crying out for you.

You need not look for me, for what would be looking is only me. You cannot approach me, because what would be approaching is only me.

Just receive my love for you in everything, and then you will know your Self.

Be Still and Know that I am God

Ramana spoke that all spiritual teaching could be summed up in one Biblical quote: "Be still and know that I am God." What does this mean?

When you are truly ready, you see through the veil of *maya,* which is everything that changes. At the center stage of maya is what has been believed to be "me." When you are still, you are not defined by a point of reference. The play of maya creates the illusion of separation born out of the experience of "me." It remains in existence because of built-in tendencies of desire and fear.

Being still means being ready not to latch onto this. You recognize there is nothing that is not the Self. The appearance of the character is the Self. The return of the experience of separation is the Self. Physical pain is the Self. Openings, closings, joy, pleasure, pain, and sorrow are all arising as maya.

The Self masquerades itself for the possibility of your home-coming. When you are ripe, you no longer care about pleasure or pain. You don't care what is going on for the character. You are not trying to break through something to an experience of pleasure. This is an ego game. When you are ripe, there is a humble conviction to receive the Beloved that is sought.

And the Beloved comes at times through veils of karma, through the separate character. This can be seen as a problem. But the separate character is an aspect of the Beloved; there never was an individual. You can only discover this when you have the fortitude to remain with whatever is going on. So long as there is a shred that is trying to make the character feel good, safe, and loved, it's impossible.

Typically during openings there is the feeling that "I am ready for anything"—because in the opening, conditioning is getting what it wants. And then it evaporates. But when you're ready, the arising and dissolving of the separate character is seen as nothing but the Self. You are ready to meet the Beloved through the face of every illusion that is possible. There is an inability to run.

There is the discovery of reality that has always been. It is not some beautiful thing that the separate character basks in. It is the realization that there has never been anything but the Beloved. And you are the stillness that has been graced to receive what the heart has longed for in the face of every single thing.

Preference becomes impossible. If there is preference, it is a reflection arising out of the Self, because the individual is a myth. It is reflecting a lack of readiness. But it is still arising in the Self. It arises directly out of what is sought, directly out of the belly of pure Love that masquerades itself, looking like pain.

What is appearing in the Self, out of pure wisdom, is direct teaching that is sculpted for the one who is ready. In this readiness is the willingness to throw one's individual life away. To throw the demon that is not there away. To remain still and receive the Beloved. Be still and know that I am God. It is time to step out of the sandbox.

What has the greatest fierceness, because it is the greatest power, is love. Love will do anything. Though the words may seem pointed, they feel like pure celebration, and they come forth because of you. The pointing is direct and honest because of something alive in you that is direct and honest. Drink it all into your cells until there are no cells left to be found.

Be still. Be still and know that I am God. This is the mystical root of all teachings.

Om Namah Shivaya. Om to the Stillness. Om to Your Self.

Biography and Contact Information

In the mystic tradition of Ramana Maharshi and Ramakrishna, Devaji offers satsang for those whose priority is freedom. With love, passion, and wisdom, he guides each seeker back home to one's true Self. Devaji lives with his wife Faith in Mt. Shasta, California, where a dedicated sangha has blossomed around him.

Each winter, he offers an extended retreat at the holy mountain of Arunachala in India and regular retreats throughout the year in California, in Mt. Shasta, the Carmel area, and the San Francisco Bay Area, as well as in Hawaii. In addition, he offers online retreats and Saturday satsangs that are available to everyone worldwide. For more information about Devaji's offerings, please visit his website, devaji.org. You can also find him on Facebook and on his Youtube channel.

* * *

Devaji's spiritual awakening erupted through the direct transmission of his guru, Sri Ramana Maharshi. This connection began with early visions of the great sage. Over time, Ramana's presence was felt almost continually, and eventually his transmission became internalized. The edges that had separated student and teacher melted into the taste of pure Oneness.

With the ground of silence firmly rooted, the ecstatic love affair of the divine heart erupted with the presence of Ramakrishna, the embodiment of pure devotion. Now the marriage of tranquility and ecstasy weave a tapestry of divine bliss.

Made in the USA
San Bernardino, CA
22 September 2018